Editor **NICK PULFORD**

Cover designed by Jay Vincent

Designed by David Dew

Richard Birch	David Jennings	Maddy Playle	Kitty Trice
Scott Burton	Nigel Jones	Lewis Porteous	Nick Watts
Tom Collins	Andrew King	James Pyman	Edward Whitaker
David Cramphorn	Jon Lees	Stuart Riley	
Graham Dench	Kevin Morley	Graeme Rodway	Fashion: Ascot
Richard Forristal	Lee Mottershead	Peter Scargill	Racecourse and
Nick Freedman	Julian Muscat	Stefan Searle	Katherine Elizabeth
Nicholas Godfrey	Justin O'Hanlon	Tom Segal	
James Hill	Dave Orton	Shane Tetley	
Pietro Innocenzi	Tom Park	Peter Thomas	

With grateful thanks to Ascot Racecourse for their invaluable assistance

Published in 2018 by Racing Post Books, 27 Kingfisher Court, Hambridge Road, Newbury RG14 5SJ
Copyright ©Racing Post 2018

ISBN 978-1-910497-52-4

Printed in Great Britain by Bishops

elcome to the Racing Post Royal Ascot 2018 Guide, the new 208-page book from the best team in the business and packed with all the information you need to get ready for the five-day summer spectacular.

This guide features an in-depth look at all 30 races across the five days, accompanied by a host of tips, betting pointers and analysis to help you find those all-important winners.

Along with profiles of the leading horses, we also have the lowdown on the top trainers and jockeys – all with handy tips on how to make money following them at Royal Ascot.

The draw, the handicaps, the trends and the international challenge are also considered by the Racing Post's team of experts as they weigh up the factors that make the difference at Flat racing's most prestigious and competitive fixture.

We don't forget the social side either, which is more important at Royal Ascot than any other race meeting, as we focus on the fashion trends, the places to see and be seen, and lots of advice on how to make the best of a day at the races.

From high society and high fashion to high-octane excitement on the track, Royal Ascot has it all. And the fun starts here.

Nick Pulford
Editor

CONTENTS

THIS IS ROYAL ASCOT

Lee Mottershead looks forward to five of the best days racing has to offer

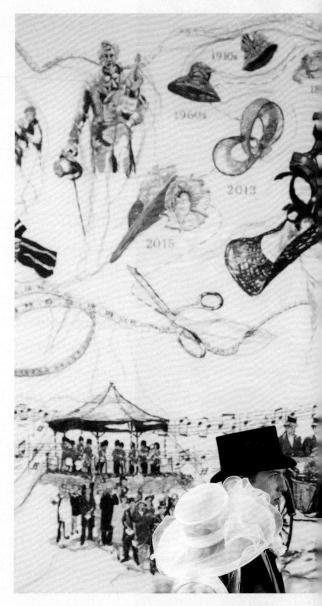

*I*t is the greatest celebration of Flat racing anywhere in the world. It is staged at the most famous racecourse in the world and plays host to some of the world's finest racehorses and riders.

Royal Ascot is a truly global occasion, yet perhaps its prime selling point is that it could not be more British.

They come from near and far, from Slough to Sydney, so they can immerse themselves in a sporting and social spectacle that simply has no equal.

For some the joy is in the pomp and the pageantry, the beauty of the royal procession and the chance to see the Queen. For some it is about the fashion. For most of us it is about the racing.

At 2pm every day royalty rolls down the track in time-honoured tradition. From 2.30pm racing royalty lights up that track.

Frankel won there, Frankie still wins there. Racegoers in their tens of thousands and television viewers in their many millions have cheered marathon marvels like Yeats and Ardross, speed machines like Black Caviar and Lady Aurelia, plus so much else. From the Queen Anne to the Queen Alexandra they will cheer again.

They will also dress to impress. Men will be in morning suits and toppers, preferably old ones made of silk. Women will be in their most elegant attire, although hats that prevent the person immediately behind from

ROYAL ASCOT

watching the Royal Hunt Cup should be discouraged.

No longer forbidden are jumpsuits, successfully introduced last year. Banned for the first time are gentlemen's ankles. In a major change to the meeting's dress code, socks are now compulsory. Ankles are still permitted but they must be covered at all times.

Over those fabulous five days, the most fabulous times are assured. What a smashing, positively dashing spectacle it will be. Royal Ascot is almost upon us.

ROYAL ASCOT ESSENTIALS

DATES

- Royal Ascot 2018 takes place over five days from Tuesday June 19 to Saturday June 23.

TICKETS

- Royal Ascot has four separate areas for racegoers and the Royal Enclosure is the most exclusive with the best views from the grandstand and by the winning post. Membership for the Royal Enclosure is by invitation only and members can book badges for themselves and their guests (day badges start at £120). A formal dress code – including full morning suit for gentlemen – applies.

- The Queen Anne Enclosure is the premier public area at Royal Ascot and provides access to the pre-parade ring, winner's enclosure and parade ring and to facilities and viewing areas on the concourse level of the grandstand. Ladies are required to wear a hat and gentlemen a matching suit and a tie. £75 Tue & Wed, £88 Thu-Sat

- The Village Enclosure, situated on the infield on the opposite side of the track from the grandstand, was introduced last year and operates on Thursday to Saturday. The aim is to create a party atmosphere with live music from 11am to 9pm, champagne and cocktail bars and eating options from boutique restaurants to street food. The dress code is less formal than in the Queen Anne Enclosure and the advice is to dress for the outdoors. Ladies are required to wear a hat and gentlemen a suit and tie. £67 Thu-Sat

- The Windsor Enclosure is located furthest up the course from the winning post and no formal dress code applies, although racegoers are encouraged to dress for the occasion. There are a range of food stalls, champagne and Pimm's bars, with live music or DJ until 7pm. Picnics are welcome subject

RACING POST

- First for Royal Ascot – web, app and newspaper
- Unrivalled cards, form, previews and tips
- Bruce Millington and the team guide you through all the action in our daily Postcasts
- Replays, results and analysis
- Live blog keeps you up to date with all the news and colour from the track from 8am daily
- Raceday Live with all the up-to-the-minute punting news and pointers
- Alastair Down heads the best reporting team in the business

to Ascot's picnic policy. £37 Tue & Wed, £46 Thu-Sat

- For more details of the dress code, see pages 88-89.

BY CAR

- **From London & the North** M4 Junction 6 onto the A332 Windsor bypass and follow the signs to Ascot.
- **From the West** M4 Junction 10 to the A329(M) signed to Bracknell and follow the signs to Ascot.
- **From the South & East** M3 Junction 3 onto the A332 signed to Bracknell and follow the signs to Ascot.
- **From the Midlands** M40 southbound, Junction 4. Take the A404 towards the M4 (Junction 8/9). On the M4 head towards Heathrow/London. Leave M4 at Junction 6 and follow the A332 Windsor bypass to Ascot.
- More than 8,000 car parking spaces are available and pre-booking is advised. Car Park 8 costs £35 per day.

BY TRAIN

- South West Trains runs a frequent service to Ascot from Reading, Guildford and London Waterloo. The average journey time is 27 minutes from Reading and 52 minutes from Waterloo. The railway station is a seven-minute walk from the racecourse.

TV DETAILS

- All 30 races will be broadcast live on ITV1 or ITV4, totalling approximately 30 hours of live coverage across the week.
- The Opening Show preview programme will be shown daily at 9.30am and coverage of the racing will start at 1.30pm.
- Racing UK is live on-air at Ascot from 9am until 6pm for each of the five days, beginning with the Mark Your Card programme.

PICNICS

- Picnics are permitted only in the Windsor Enclosure. They must be carried in a picnic hamper or coolbag/box and sharp-bladed kitchen knives are not permitted. Each customer (over the age of 18) is allowed to bring one bottle of sparkling wine or champagne to accompany their picnic (no other type of alcohol can be brought in).
- Blankets and fold-up chairs are permitted, again only in the Windsor Enclosure, and private picnic benches, seating six, can be pre-booked in the Windsor Enclosure at a cost of £120.
- Royal Enclosure, Queen Anne Enclosure and Village Enclosure guests can picnic only in the car and coach parks. No food, drinks or snacks can be taken into those enclosures.
- A range of picnics can be pre-ordered, priced from £95 for Royal, Queen Anne and Village Enclosure guests and from £57.50 for the Windsor Enclosure.

Ladbrokes

JOIN THE GRID

Track your bet, cash out & collect cash in-shop with The Grid

DOWNLOAD THE GRID APP

DAY ONE

*R*oyal Ascot roars in like a lion with three Group 1 races on the opening day – all in the first four races. The action comes thick and fast, creating an immediate buzz around the track with racing from the very top drawer.

Only British Champions Day at Ascot in October can top three Group 1 races on the same card and the Tuesday action at the royal meeting starts at the highest level with the Queen Anne Stakes, a Group 1 mile race for four-year-olds and up with an illustrious roll of honour headed by 2012 winner Frankel.

This contest often draws an international cast, with victories for Ireland, France and the United States as well as Britain in recent years, and provides a blockbuster opening to the week.

The second course on the menu is the Group 2 Coventry Stakes, the premier race for two-year-olds at the meeting and often the first proving ground for budding champions and next year's Classic contenders. Four of the winners since 2007 went on to Classic success the following year in the 2,000 Guineas at Newmarket or the Irish 2,000 Guineas.

Next up is the fastest race of the week as the top sprinters take centre stage for the blink-and-you'll-miss-it five-furlong dash of the King's Stand Stakes. Last year Lady Aurelia covered the distance at speeds in excess of 40mph and stopped the clock at a phenomenal 57.45sec, just 0.01sec outside the track record.

The Classic milers – many of whom will be coming from Guineas assignments in Britain, Ireland and France – go head-to-head in the St James's Palace Stakes. Whereas the Queen Anne is run on the straight mile, this contest races around the bend and positioning can be vital before the final run up Ascot's relatively short straight.

After that whirlwind of activity, there might just be time to catch your breath and perhaps a glass of something chilled before the final two races of the afternoon.

Ascot's variety is evident with the switch to long distance in the Ascot Stakes, a handicap run over the marathon trip of two and a half miles. The distance is then halved for the final race, the Listed Wolferton Stakes, which has been moved from its previous Saturday slot.

Tuesday June 19

RUNNING ORDER

2.30 Queen Anne Stakes (Group 1) *Last year's winner: Ribchester 11-10f*	**1m** 4yo+	£600,000
3.05 Coventry Stakes (Group 2) *Last year's winner: Rajasinghe 11-1*	**6f** 2yo	£150,000
3.40 King's Stand Stakes (Group 1) *Last year's winner: Lady Aurelia 7-2*	**5f** 3yo+	£500,000
4.20 St James's Palace Stakes (Group 1) *Last year's winner: Barney Roy 5-2*	**1m** 3yo colts	£500,000
5.00 Ascot Stakes (Handicap) *Last year's winner: Thomas Hobson 4-1f*	**2m4f** 4yo+	£90,000
5.35 Wolferton Stakes (Listed) *Last year's winner: Snoano 25-1*	**1m2f** 4yo+	£100,000

Race value is total prize-money

Ribchester: last year's Queen Anne winner landed the Lockinge en route

This is the meeting's top mile race for older horses (aged four and up) and in terms of quality last year's edition won by Ribchester ranked second only to the Prince of Wales's Stakes as the best contest of Royal Ascot.

That quality is reflected in the fact that nine of the last ten winners came into the race with an adjusted Racing Post Rating of at least 134 and already with Group 1 success on their record. The exception to that rule in both cases was 2013 winner Declaration Of War, who had run in a Group 1 last time (fifth in the Lockinge) but was yet to win above Group 3 level.

After a couple of five-year-old winners in 2015 and 2016, Ribchester marked a return to the norm

Story of the last ten years

	FORM	WINNER	AGE & WGT	Adj RPR	SP	TRAINER	BEST RPR LAST 12 MONTHS (RUNS SINCE)
17	12-31	**Ribchester** C, D	4 9-0	139^T	11-10f	Richard Fahey	won Lockinge Stakes Gp1 (1m) (0)
16	-11J1	**Tepin** D	5 8-11	138^T	11-2	Mark Casse (CAN)	won Keeneland Gd1 (1m½f) (1)
15	1-111	**Solow** D	5 9-0	139^{-2}	11-8f	Freddy Head (FR)	won Dubai Turf Gp1 (1m1f) (1)
14	4216-	**Toronado** C, D	4 9-0	143^T	4-5f	Richard Hannon	won Sussex Stakes Gp1 (1m) (1)
13	11-15	**Declaration Of War** D, BF	4 9-0	128^{-11}	15-2	Aidan O'Brien (IRE)	won Leopardstown Listed (1m) (1)
12	111-1	**Frankel** D	4 9-0	153^T	1-10f	Sir Henry Cecil	won Lockinge Stakes Gp1 (1m) (0)
11	111-1	**Canford Cliffs** C, D	4 9-0	144^T	11-8	Richard Hannon snr	won Sussex Stakes Gp1 (1m) (1)
10	131-1	**Goldikova** D	5 8-11	148^T	11-8f	Freddy Head (FR)	won Prix Jacques le Marois Gp1 (1m) (3)
09	1-814	**Paco Boy** D, BF	4 9-0	141^{-2}	10-3	Richard Hannon Snr	won Prix de la Foret Gp1 (7f) (3)
08	330-6	**Haradasun** D	5 9-0	134^{-7}	5-1	Aidan O'Brien (IRE)	2nd Moonee Valley Gp2 (1m) (4)

WINS-PL-RUNS 4yo 6-11-50, 5yo 4-6-34, 6yo+ 0-3-24 **FAVOURITES** -£0.25

TRAINERS IN THIS RACE (w-pl-r) Aidan O'Brien 2-4-13, Richard Hannon 1-0-7, Richard Fahey 1-0-3, Charlie Hills 0-0-2, David Simcock 0-1-3, Graham Motion 0-0-2, Jane Chapple-Hyam 0-0-2, Roger Varian 0-2-4, William Haggas 0-2-2

FATE OF FAVOURITES 3612101121 **POSITION OF WINNER IN MARKET** 2212121131

2.30 Queen Anne Stakes

as he became the 13th four-year-old to land the race in 18 runnings since 2000 (all the others were five). He was also the eighth winner for Godolphin, leading owner in the race's history, but the first since Ramonti in 2007 and the first not trained by Saeed Bin Suroor, whose seven victories make him the leading trainer.

Ribchester also had the right sort of profile as a three-year-old, having run well in a Guineas (third in the 2,000 at Newmarket) and at Royal Ascot (won the Jersey Stakes). Seven of the 13 four-year-old winners since 2000 fitted one of those criteria, with a top-three finish in a Guineas (three won) or in the St James's Palace Stakes (two won). Most of the other four-year-old winners were late developers or had been held up by injury the previous year, with four of them having missed the Guineas and Royal Ascot. The Lockinge is the key

The mighty Frankel storms to victory in the 2012 Queen Anne – one of 14 wins during his phenomenal track career

Key trends
▶ *Aged four or five, ten winners in ten runnings*
▶ *Distance winner, 10/10*
▶ *Ran earlier that year, 9/10 (eight had won)*
▶ *Adjusted Racing Post Rating of at least 134, 9/10*
▶ *Rated within 7lb of RPR top-rated, 9/10*
▶ *Group 1 winner, 9/10*

Other factors
▶ *Five winners were trained by the Hannon yard or Aidan O'Brien. Three of the other five were trained in France or America*
▶ *Six winners had run in the Lockinge, in which they finished 641151; six Lockinge winners ran, finishing 211521*

DID YOU KNOW?
Since Queen Anne founded Ascot racecourse in 1711, a further 11 monarchs have acceded to the British throne

stepping stone, with the last seven British-trained winners having run in the Newbury Group 1 (finishing 8241111) and Aidan O'Brien's last two winners having prepped there (finishing 65). The US-trained Tepin in 2016 is the only one of the last 11 winners who had not run in a Group 1 last time (a Grade 2 at Churchill Downs in her case) – the three French-trained winners had all run in the Prix d'Ispahan.

In recent years the yards to note have been Ballydoyle and the Hannon stable. Since 2008 with fancied runners (below 10-1) the form figures for Aidan O'Brien are 166212 and for the Hannons they are 121154. The recent French record is good, with three wins and five places from 15 runners since 2005.

The top of the market is the place to concentrate. The last 11 winners have come from the first three in the betting and the last winner bigger than 15-2 was Refuse To Bend (12-1) in 2004.

QUEEN ANNE STAKES

SUPERSTAR WINNER

Frankel (2012)

Perhaps the greatest racehorse of all time, with a modern-day record official rating of 140; unbeaten in 14 starts, ten of which came at G1 level; won five races at Ascot in total, including the G1 St James's Palace Stakes, the G1 Queen Elizabeth II Stakes and the G1 Champion Stakes. His Queen Anne Stakes performance was breathtaking, making all to win by 11 lengths

BETTING

Longest-priced winner: Alflora 20-1 (1993)

Shortest-priced winner: Frankel 1-10 (2012)

Market leaders: 20 favourites or joint favourites have been successful in 72 runnings

FROM THE ARCHIVES

A remarkable running in 1974 saw the first three horses home – Confusion, Gloss and Royal Prerogative – disqualified for causing interference, with the race awarded to the Italian challenger Brook, who went past the post in fourth for trainer Mario Benetti and jockey Brian Taylor

* All figures since 1946

WINNING CONNECTIONS

Most successful trainer
7 wins: Saeed Bin Suroor
Charnwood Forest (1996)
Allied Forces (1997)
Intikhab (1998)
Cape Cross (1999)
Dubai Destination (2003)
Refuse To Bend (2004)
Ramonti (2007)

Most successful jockey
6 wins: Frankie Dettori
Markofdistinction (1990)
Allied Forces (1997)
Intikhab (1998)
Dubai Destination (2003)
Refuse To Bend (2004)
Ramonti (2007)

Most successful owner
8 wins: Godolphin
Charnwod Forest (1996)
Allied Forces (1997)
Intikhab (1998)
Cape Cross (1999)
Dubai Destination (2003)
Refuse To Bend (2004)
Ramonti (2007)
Ribchester (2017)

This 6f contest is the most valuable race for juveniles at Royal Ascot and the season's first high-class contest for the age group, regularly proving a stepping stone to Group 1 level later in the year.

One run is often enough to prepare for this test, as it was for 11-1 winner Rajasinghe *(pictured)* last year and eight others in the past 20 years (only three winners in that period had run more than twice).

All of those once-raced juveniles had won, and indeed just five of the last 20 winners had suffered a defeat before Ascot. The last winner to arrive off the back of a last-time-out defeat was Harbour Master in 1997.

Just four of the last 20 winners had scored only at 5f, pointing to winning form over 6f (or even 7f) being important in preparation for Ascot's stiff test.

Key races to check out are the National Stakes at Sandown, the Woodcote Stakes at Epsom, the Marble Hill Stakes at the Curragh, Gowran Park 7f races and Newbury May maidens. It is also worth noting the last three winners all started their careers on the all-weather.

Market position is a good guide, with 12 of the last 20 winners having been first or second favourite and only three of those 20 priced above 8-1 (one was Rajasinghe last year and the other two were 20-1 shots for Aidan O'Brien, the top trainer with eight victories).

Key trends
▶ *Lost maiden tag, 10/10*
▶ *Won last time out, 10/10*
▶ *Rated within 4lb of RPR top-rated, 8/10 (seven were top-rated)*
▶ *Adjusted RPR of at least 110, 8/10*
▶ *Won a previous start by at least two lengths, 8/10*
▶ *Distance winner, 7/10*
▶ *By a sire with a stamina index between 7.1f and 9.9f, 6/10*

Other factors
▶ *Nine winners came here undefeated. Buratino, who won in 2015, had been beaten twice over 5f but was undefeated over 6f*
▶ *Last year's winner Rajasinghe returned at 11-1 and War Command obliged at 20-1 in 2013, but the other eight winners were single-figure odds, including five favourites (one joint)*

Story of the last ten years

FORM		WINNER	AGE & WGT	Adj RPR	SP	TRAINER	BEST RPR LAST 12 MONTHS (RUNS SINCE)
17	1	**Rajasinghe** D	2 9-1	103^{-13}	11-1	Richard Spencer	won Newcastle Class 4 nov (6f) (0)
16	11	**Caravaggio**	2 9-1	119^{T}	13-8f	Aidan O'Brien (IRE)	won Curragh Listed (5f) (0)
15	13121	**Buratino** D	2 9-1	118^{T}	6-1	Mark Johnston	won Woodcote Stakes Listed (6f) (0)
14	1	**The Wow Signal** D	2 9-1	110^{-4}	5-1j	John Quinn	won Ayr Class 4 mdn (6f) (0)
13	1	**War Command** D	2 9-1	104^{-12}	20-1	Aidan O'Brien (IRE)	won Leopardstown mdn (7f) (0)
12	111	**Dawn Approach** D	2 9-1	118^{T}	7-2	Jim Bolger (IRE)	won Naas Listed (6f) (0)
11	11	**Power** D	2 9-1	117^{T}	4-1f	Aidan O'Brien (IRE)	won Curragh Listed (5f) (0)
10	1	**Strong Suit** D	2 9-1	113^{T}	15-8f	Richard Hannon snr	won Newbury Class 4 mdn (6f) (0)
09	1	**Canford Cliffs** D	2 9-1	112^{-T}	7-4f	Richard Hannon snr	won Newbury Class 4 mdn (6f) (0)
08	11	**Art Connoisseur** D	2 9-1	115^{-T}	8-1	Michael Bell	won Newmarket Class 3 (5f) (0)

FAVOURITES £6.25 **TRAINERS IN THIS RACE** (w-pl-r) Aidan O'Brien 3-4-15, Mark Johnston 1-1-13, Brian Meehan 0-2-6, Charlie Hills 0-0-6, Charlie Appleby 0-0-3, Clive Cox 0-1-4, Richard Hannon 0-2-8, Wesley Ward 0-0-3, William Haggas 0-1-3

FATE OF FAVOURITES 5111461014 **POSITION OF WINNER IN MARKET** 3111291316

This 5f contest for three-year-olds and up is the fastest race of the week, usually completed in less than a minute, and Lady Aurelia went close to the record last year in winning by three lengths in 57.45sec. It was a remarkable performance by the only three-year-old in the field and it may be some years before we see another of her ilk.

Three-year-olds always struggled to win at this high level so early in the season and, with the advent of the Group 1 Commonwealth Cup for that age group, many of the best young sprinters are bypassing this race. That is only going to reinforce the trend towards older winners, with ten of the last 14 renewals claimed by horses aged five or above.

Australia won four of the seven runnings from 2003 to 2009 but their wave of success has ebbed and six of the last eight have gone to Britain or Ireland, with Hong Kong (Little Bridge in 2012) and the United States (Lady Aurelia) providing the most recent winners from outside Europe.

Those last six winners from Britain and Ireland had contested the Palace House Stakes at Newmarket or the Temple Stakes at Haydock (and frequently both) that season and five of them had

Story of the last ten years

FORM		WINNER	AGE & WGT	Adj RPR	SP	TRAINER	BEST RPR LAST 12 MONTHS (RUNS SINCE)
17	113-1	**Lady Aurelia** CD	3 8-9	138^T	7-2	Wesley Ward (USA)	won Keeneland Listed (5½f) (0)
16	05-11	**Profitable** D	4 9-4	131^{-3}	4-1	Clive Cox	won Temple Stakes Gp2 (5f) (0)
15	42-17	**Goldream** CD	6 9-4	125^{-6}	20-1	Robert Cowell	won Palace House Stakes Gp3 (5f) (1)
14	2-471	**Sole Power** CD	7 9-4	130^T	5-1	Eddie Lynam (IRE)	won King's Stand Stakes Gp1 (5f) (7)
13	-2414	**Sole Power** D, BF	6 9-4	127^{-6}	8-1	Eddie Lynam (IRE)	won Palace House Stakes Gp3 (5f) (1)
12	-7611	**Little Bridge** D	6 9-4	132^{-1}	12-1	Danny Shum (HK)	won Sha Tin Listed hcap (5f) (1)
11	59432	**Prohibit** CD	6 9-4	126^{-6}	7-1	Robert Cowell	2nd Prix du Gros-Chene Gp2 (5f) (0)
10	0-112	**Equiano** CD, BF	5 9-4	129^{-4}	9-2	Barry Hills	2nd Temple Stakes Gp2 (5f) (0)
09	-2151	**Scenic Blast** D	5 9-4	131^T	11-4f	Daniel Morton (AUS)	won Flemington Gd1 hcap (6f) (0)
08	3-212	**Equiano**	3 8-12	123^{-14}	22-1	M Delcher Sanchez (FR)	2nd Prix du Gros-Chene Gp2 (5f) (0)

WINS-PL-RUNS 3yo 2-3-23, 4yo 1-5-35, 5yo 1-6-31, 6yo+ 6-6-67 **FAVOURITES** -£6.25

TRAINERS IN THIS RACE (w-pl-r) Robert Cowell 2-0-9, Wesley Ward 1-0-3, Clive Cox 1-1-5, Aidan O'Brien 0-0-3, Bryan Smart 0-0-7, Charlie Hills 0-1-3, David C Griffiths 0-0-4, Jeremy Gask 0-1-6, William Muir 0-1-5, William Haggas 0-1-5

FATE OF FAVOURITES 3166023503 **POSITION OF WINNER IN MARKET** 8134543822

won at least one of those contests (the other was third) – a win in the Palace House seems to count for more, with five of the last eight to attempt the double having been successful (compared with only one of the last eight Temple winners to try).

Significant races from further afield are the Prix du Gros-Chene (The Tatling in 2004, Equiano in 2008 and Prohibit in 2011 all placed before coming here) and the Prix de Saint-Georges, won by French-trained Chineur before his King's Stand victory in 2005 (Prohibit was fourth in 2011).

Group 1-winning form is important with overseas raiders (all four Australian winners and Lady Aurelia qualified, with Hong Kong's Little Bridge an exception)

Key trends
▶ *Adjusted RPR of at least 123, 10/10*
▶ *Rated within 6lb of RPR top-rated, 9/10*
▶ *Won that season, 9/10*
▶ *Group winner over 5f, 8/10*
▶ *Drawn seven or higher, 8/10*
▶ *Ran at least three times that season, 7/10 (last three winners the exceptions)*

Other factors
▶ *There has been only one winning favourite in the past ten years*
▶ *Six beaten favourites had won a Group race last time (includes both joint-favourites from 2012)*
▶ *The record of Palace House winners is 01011113; Temple Stakes 3268203410. Britain and Ireland have had six of the last eight winners, five of whom ran in the Temple, finishing 23471*

Lady Aurelia: Wesley Ward's speedster blitzes home to win last year's King's Stand

DID YOU KNOW?
The racecourse has 163 full-time staff, which increases by more than 6,500 temporary staff during Royal Ascot

but not so much for the British and Irish (three of the last six were scoring for the first time at this level). A good level of Group form is virtually a must, however.

Favourites can be found out (only two of the last 23 have won) but the market is still a good guide. Since Choisir's 25-1 win in 2003, at a time when the strength of the Australian challenge was underestimated, 11 of the 14 winners have been no bigger than 8-1 and eight of those came from the top three in the betting.

DAY ONE

This is the third Group 1 of a stupendous opening day and often brings together the Guineas principals from Britain, Ireland and France for an early sorting out of the three-year-old colts' miling division.

Only two of the last 20 winners had not run in a Guineas and that pair had both run in a French Group 1 last time out (Dr Fong was third in the Prix Jean Prat in 1998 and Most Improved was 14th in the French Derby in 2012).

Thirteen of the 18 who had run in a Guineas in that period had enjoyed Classic success (some in more than one of them) and four more had been runner-up, with the worst position being Excellent Art's fourth in the French Guineas in 2007.

Three of the last eight St James's Palace winners – Canford Cliffs (2010), Kingman (2014) and Barney Roy (2017) – reversed form after a Guineas defeat at Newmarket. The first two of those had preceded Ascot success with Guineas victory in Ireland, while Barney Roy had not run in between. Mastercraftsman in 2009 also reversed Newmarket form with the best performer from that Classic (winner Sea The Stars did not run at Ascot, having gone on to win the Derby instead).

Eleven of the last 20 winners had run in both the Newmarket and Irish Guineas and only two of those went backwards on the second run in terms of their finishing position (Zafeen was 14th in Ireland after being runner-up at Newmarket in 2003 and Galileo Gold went from first to second in 2016).

Of the seven who did not win at Newmarket, four stepped up to first place in Ireland.

Not surprisingly, given his tremendous strength in depth in the Classics division, Aidan O'Brien has won seven of the last 18 runnings. Between them, his seven winners had run in 13 Guineas with form figures of 2261114115111 – five of them had won a Guineas and three had done the Newmarket/Irish Guineas double.

The preponderance of strong Guineas form means favourites have a good record, with 12 winning in the past 20 years.

No winner has been bigger than 9-1 in that period and only one (Black Minnaloushe in 2001) came from outside the top four in the betting. The last shock winner was Brief Truce at 25-1 in 1992.

4.20 St James's Palace Stakes

Barney Roy lands last year's St James's Palace Stakes under a delighted James Doyle

Key trends

▶ Had made the frame in a Group 1, 10/10
▶ Rated within 7lb of RPR top-rated, 10/10 (eight were top-rated)
▶ Adjusted RPR of at least 130, 10/10
▶ Had finished in the first three in a 2,000 Guineas, 9/10
▶ From the first three in the market, 9/10

Other factors

▶ Winners who had run in a Guineas finished 153112112 at Newmarket and 111112 at the Curragh
▶ The last winner to run in the French Guineas was Excellent Art in 2007
▶ Six winners had run in the British and Irish Guineas with all making the frame in both
▶ Record of Guineas winners: Newmarket 17112114; Irish 111091134. The last winner not to have run in a Group 1 that season was Shavian in 1990

Story of the last ten years

FORM	WINNER	AGE	& WGT	Adj RPR	SP	TRAINER	BEST RPR LAST 12 MONTHS (RUNS SINCE)
17 1-12	Barney Roy C, D	3	9-0	132-7	5-2	Richard Hannon	2nd 2,000 Guineas Gp1 (1m) (0)
16 13-12	Galileo Gold D, BF	3	9-0	137T	6-1	Hugo Palmer	won 2,000 Guineas Gp1 (1m) (1)
15 11d-11	Gleneagles D	3	9-0	137T	8-15f	Aidan O'Brien (IRE)	won 2,000 Guineas Gp1 (1m) (1)
14 1-121	Kingman D	3	9-0	140T	8-11f	John Gosden	won Irish 2,000 Guineas Gp1 (1m) (0)
13 11-10	Dawn Approach C, D, BF	3	9-0	141T	5-4f	Jim Bolger (IRE)	won 2,000 Guineas Gp1 (1m) (1)
12 213-0	Most Improved	3	9-0	130-2	9-1	Brian Meehan	3rd Dewhurst Stakes Gp1 (7f) (1)
11 11-11	Frankel CD	3	9-0	147T30-100f		Sir Henry Cecil	won 2,000 Guineas Gp1 (1m) (1)
10 3-231	Canford Cliffs C, D	3	9-0	140T	11-4j	Richard Hannon snr	won Irish 2,000 Guineas Gp1 (1m) (0)
09 14-51	Mastercraftsman D	3	9-0	136T	5-6f	Aidan O'Brien (IRE)	won Irish 2,000 Guineas Gp1 (1m) (0)
08 23-11	Henrythenavigator C, D	3	9-0	140T	4-7f	Aidan O'Brien (IRE)	won Irish 2,000 Guineas Gp1 (1m) (0)

FAVOURITES £2.09 **TRAINERS IN THIS RACE (w-pl-r)** Aidan O'Brien 3-4-20, Richard Hannon 1-1-3, Richard Fahey 0-0-3, Saeed Bin Suroor 0-1-3, William Haggas 0-0-2 **FATE OF FAVOURITES** 1111011124 **POSITION OF WINNER IN MARKET** 1111411132

ST JAMES'S PALACE STAKES

STAR WINNERS

Tudor Minstrel (1947)
Eight-length victor of the 2,000 Guineas despite being eased down, the biggest winning distance in the race's history

Brigadier Gerard (1971)
Won 17 of his 18 career starts over distances from five furlongs to a mile and a half; unbeaten in five starts at Ascot

Frankel (2011)
Unbeaten in 14 starts, ten of which came at G1 level; won again at the royal meeting in 2012 in the Queen Anne Stakes

BETTING

Longest-priced winner: Brief Truce 25-1 (1992)

Shortest-priced winner: Venture VII 1-33 (1960)

Market leaders: 35 favourites or joint favourites have been successful in 72 runnings

CLASSIC HEROES

Guineas winners who went on to land the St James's Palace

Galileo Gold

English 14 Most recent: Galileo Gold (2016)

Irish 12 Most recent: Gleneagles (2015)

French 3 Most recent: Shamardal (2005)

All figures since 1946

WINNING CONNECTIONS

Most successful trainer
7 wins: Aidan O'Brien
Giant's Causeway (2000)
Black Minnaloushe (2001)
Rock Of Gibraltar (2002)
Excellent Art (2007)
Henrythenavigator (2008)
Mastercraftsman (2009)
Gleneagles (2015)

Most successful jockey
6 wins: Mick Kinane
Dara Monarch (1982)
Brief Truce (1992)
Grand Lodge (1994)
Giant's Causeway (2000)
Rock Of Gibraltar (2002)
Azamour (2004)

Most successful owner
7 wins: Coolmore partners
Giant's Causeway (2000)
Black Minnaloushe (2001)
Rock Of Gibraltar (2002)
Excellent Art (2007)
Henrythenavigator (2008)
Mastercraftsman (2009)
Gleneagles (2015)

The long-distance races are an important part of Royal Ascot's heritage and this 2m4f handicap, founded in 1839, is the first of four races at the meeting in which the field passes the winning post twice.

Trainers whose main emphasis is jump racing have dominated this contest in recent years, with Irish-based handlers responsible for five of the last six winners.

Willie Mullins has claimed three of those successes – with Simenon in 2012, Clondaw Warrior in 2015 and Thomas Hobson last year – and his record in that period from seven runners is 1017701 for a level-stake profit of +13pt. A favourite Mullins tactic is to attempt to double up in the Queen Alexandra Stakes (the final race on Saturday) – he did it with Simenon and just fell

short with Thomas Hobson, who was second on the Saturday.

Other notable jumps trainers to win include Nicky Henderson, Jonjo O'Neill, David Pipe (and his father Martin on four occasions) and Tony Martin (twice).

The last Newmarket trainer to win was Jane Chapple-Hyam with Judgethemoment in 2009 and before that it was Sir Michael Stoute with Cover Up in 2001.

Nine of the last 14 winners have been in a fairly narrow weights range from 8st 12lb to 9st 3lb, but a heavier burden is not a barrier to success with three winners and one runner-up carrying top weight of 9st 10lb

in the six runnings since 2012.

The market is a good guide, with eight of the last ten winners coming from the top four in the betting.

Key trends
▶ *Raced no more than twice on the Flat that season, 10/10*
▶ *Officially rated 85-95, 9/10*
▶ *Won a Flat handicap, 9/10 (exception was Group placed)*
▶ *Previously ran over hurdles, 9/10*
▶ *Won within their last three Flat starts, 8/10*
▶ *Carried between 9st and 9st 7lb, 7/10 (all three exceptions carried top weight of 9st 10lb)*

Other factors
▶ *Only two winners had scored beyond 2m on the Flat*

Thomas Hobson gives Willie Mullins a third Ascot Stakes victory

Story of the last ten years

FORM		WINNER	AGE & WGT	OR	SP	TRAINER	BEST RPR LAST 12 MONTHS (RUNS SINCE)
17	1211/	**Thomas Hobson**	7 9-10	100ᵀ	4-1f	Willie Mullins (IRE)	Seasonal debut (0)
16	/21-1	**Jennies Jewel**	9 9-3	93⁻⁴	6-1	Jarlath Fahey (IRE)	won Curragh hcap (2m) (0)
15	2101-	**Clondaw Warrior**	8 9-0	89⁻⁴	5-1f	Willie Mullins (IRE)	won Leopardstown hcap (1m7f) (0)
14	120-0	**Domination**	7 9-7	92⁻³	12-1	Charles Byrnes (IRE)	2nd Galway hcap (2m) (2)
13	086/1	**Well Sharp**	5 9-10	95⁻⁶	9-1	Jonjo O'Neill	won York Class 3 hcap (2m½f) (0)
12	/350-	**Simenon**	5 9-10	95ᵀ	8-1	Willie Mullins (IRE)	14th Newcastle Class 2 hcap (2m) (0)
11	/70-1	**Veiled**	5 9-3	88⁻¹	11-2	Nicky Henderson	won Newmarket Class 4 hcap (1m6f) (0)
10	/131/	**Junior**	7 9-0	85ᵀ	17-2	David Pipe	Seasonal debut (0)
09	66-11	**Judgethemoment** C	4 9-5	91⁻²	13-2	Jane Chapple-Hyam	won Ascot Class 3 hcap (2m) (0)
08	41-04	**Missoula**	5 9-0	85⁻⁴	20-1	Suzy Smith	won York Class 3 hcap (2m2f) (2)

WINS-PL-RUNS 4yo 1-12-45, 5yo 4-9-64, 6yo+ 5-10-83 **FAVOURITES** £1.00

FATE OF FAVOURITES 3044025101 POSITION OF **WINNER IN MARKET** 9233347121

Ladbrokes

£5K GUARANTEE

WE GUARANTEE TO LAY ANY HORSE TO LOSE AT LEAST £5,000

Available In-Shop on all live ITV races and other selected races

DOWNLOAD THE APP

5.35 Wolferton Stakes

naugurated in 2002 with the extension of Royal Ascot to a five-day meeting, this race has been a 1m2f Listed handicap for four-year-olds and older until now but has been changed this year.

Following consultation with the BHA Flat Pattern Committee, the Wolferton now becomes a straight Listed race – over the same distance and for the same age group – and the Sandringham (which was also a Listed handicap) becomes a regular handicap.

The Wolferton as a non-handicap has been moved to Tuesday from Saturday, in order to maximise the distance between it and the Listed Gala Stakes at Sandown.

The alteration in status might bring some changes to the winning profile, but it seems safe to say this race will continue to be targeted by the top trainers for their later-maturing, well-bred types. Aidan O'Brien won two years ago with Sir Isaac Newton and six of the previous seven runnings went to Newmarket trainers.

John Gosden has the best record with three winners, while Sir Michael Stoute and the late Michael Jarvis – also based in Newmarket – saddled two apiece.

Key trends
▶ *Aged four or five, 9/10 (seven aged four)*
▶ *Won at Class 3 level or higher, 8/10*
▶ *Ran no more than twice that season, 8/10*
▶ *Beaten on previous start, 8/10 (four over a different distance to this race)*
▶ *Finished in the top six last time out, 8/10 (one exception had finished runner-up over hurdles last time)*
▶ *Drawn in single figures, 8/10*

Other factors
▶ *John Gosden has won three times*

Delighted connections after Snoano's 25-1 win in last year's Wolferton

Story of the last ten years

FORM		WINNER	AGE & WGT	Adj RPR	SP	TRAINER	BEST RPR LAST 12 MONTHS (RUNS SINCE)
17	8-157	**Snoano** D	5 9-0	120-4	25-1	Tim Easterby	5th Chester Gp3 (1m2½f) (1)
16	64-23	**Sir Issac Newton**	4 9-0	122T	7-1	Aidan O'Brien (IRE)	4th Leopardstown Gp2 (1m) (2)
15	1-11	**Mahsoob** D	4 9-3	124-1	7-4f	John Gosden	won York Class 2 hcap (1m2½f) (0)
14	24-13	**Contributer** D	4 9-5	116-6	9-1	Ed Dunlop	won Kempton Listed (1m2f) (1)
13	5750/	**Forgotten Voice** C	8 9-2	124T	12-1	Nicky Henderson	Seasonal debut (0)
12	14-11	**Gatewood** D	4 8-11	124T	3-1f	John Gosden	won Epsom Class 2 hcap (1m2f) (0)
11	1-523	**Beachfire** D, BF	4 8-9	123-2	12-1	John Gosden	3rd Goodwood Class 2 hcap (1m4f) (0)
10	111-2	**Rainbow Peak** CD, BF	4 9-4	124T	13-8f	Michael Jarvis	2nd Hambleton Stakes Listed hcap (1m) (0)
09	60-16	**Perfect Stride** C	4 9-5	122-5	8-1	Sir Michael Stoute	won Ascot Listed (1m) (1)
08	90-43	**Supaseus** C	5 8-11	121-5	12-1	Hughie Morrison	3rd York Class 2 hcap (1m2½f) (0)

WINS-RUNS 4yo 7-13-62, 5yo 2-3-41, 6yo+ 1-5-36 **FAVOURITES** -£0.63

FATE OF FAVOURITES 6010152160 **POSITION OF WINNER IN MARKET** 6315174140

Leading our field.

**To find out what gives us the edge,
ask your broker about Markel International**

Specialist insurance

FIVE OF THE BEST . . .

CREAM RISES

Royal Ascot is Flat racing's equivalent of the Cheltenham Festival. Ninety-nine per cent of the participants have been primed to peak at this meeting and every race is fiercely competitive. I always keep my stakes lower than I would at other fixtures to reflect this, but often back two or three horses in the big-runner handicaps such as the Wokingham and Royal Hunt Cup. It's a meeting where class is paramount and, given good or faster going, the cream usually rises to the top.

Richard Birch

HIGH DRAW BEST

Many hold the belief that a low draw close to the inside rail is preferred in big fields over 1m4f at Ascot but the results of the King George V Handicap and the Duke of Edinburgh Handicap suggest the opposite is true. In those handicaps going back to 1998 (omitting the meeting held at York in 2005), 103 of the 152 horses to reach the first four were drawn in double figures, providing 31 of the 38 winners. If you had concentrated on those whose SP was no bigger than 10-1, you would have found 21 winners with a 19 per cent strike-rate, returning a level-stake profit of +52.75pt.

Kevin Morley

KEEP IT SIMPLE

The first four races on the opening day are arguably the most punter-friendly bunch of the week, so don't overcomplicate things. Fourteen of the last 16 Queen Anne winners were 13-2 or shorter; 13 of the last 16 Coventry winners came from the first three in the betting; 11 of the last 16 King's Stand winners were 8-1 or shorter; all bar one of the last 16 St James's Palace winners was 8-1 or shorter. That all suggests you should narrow down these races when it comes to studying the form.

Pietro Innocenzi

Punting pointers

DON'T FORGET SIRE STUDY

Punters traditionally use trainer form or jockey form as a way of finding a way into any race at Royal Ascot but you never hear anyone talk about sire form. Ascot is a very different surface up the straight to anywhere else in the country and American-bred sires, in particular War Front and latterly Scat Daddy, have enjoyed plenty of success at the royal meeting. Scat Daddy died too early but if you had backed all eight Royal Ascot runners he sired last year you would have found four winners, including one at 20-1 and one at 14-1, and another couple of placed horses at big prices as well. Scat Daddy's son No Nay Never, who is standing at Coolmore and has his first two-year-olds this year, strikes me as the heir apparent and anything sired by him might well have an in-built advantage at Ascot. **Tom Segal**

JOCKEY BOOKINGS

If there is one thing that can guarantee a horse will be a bigger price than it should be, it is when the stable jockey has jumped off to ride something else. While I have plenty of respect for Ryan Moore, who has the pick of the Aidan O'Brien runners, he will almost always get one decision wrong over the week and that's the time to cash in with the supposed second string, usually ridden by Seamie Heffernan. He has been successful only four times from 38 rides at the meeting since 2006, but the winners were 20-1, 20-1, 16-1 and 9-2 and a £1 bet on all of his rides in that period would have yielded a profit of £26.50. **Graeme Rodway**

A huge crowd watches the 2016 Albany Stakes, won by the Aidan O'Brien-trained Brave Anna at 16-1 and ridden by Seamie Heffernan. O'Brien's other runner in the race – 2-1 Cuff, ridden by Ryan Moore – was fifth

HAVE SOME DRESS SENSE

Ascot's strict dress code is one thing, but there are some sensible rules worth following for any visitor. Number one for many people is to wear sensible shoes (or at least pack a lightweight pair) – you'll be on your feet all day and there's a lot of walking. The British summer is so unpredictable that precautions from sunscreen to an umbrella might be required. But let's not forget dressing up is a big part of the occasion – the best advice is to keep it classy.

Survival tips

DO SOME RESEARCH

Ascot is vast and so are the crowds, and a little preparation goes a long way in helping you get around. Choose the enclosure that suits you, decide what you want to see and when (you might want to watch the horses from several different vantage points during the day) and check out the details on the racecourse website. And don't forget your copy of the Racing Post to help you find those all-important winners.

SET A BUDGET

Royal Ascot is an indulgent treat but you don't have to keep up with the Smyth-Jones's. It's just as much fun to bring your own picnic – few things are more pleasant on a warm June afternoon. On the betting front, decide how much you want to risk on each of the six races at the start of the day and resist the temptation to up your stakes if you hit a losing run.

ARRIVE IN TIME

Traffic to the course is always a nightmare, so set off early – best of all, nominate someone else as the designated driver. Trains are packed too, and an early start might ease the crush. Remember there's plenty to see once you get there, so you won't be bored, and being an early bird enables you to nab a good spot for a picnic or to see the royal procession.

PLAY THE LONG GAME

It's going to be a long day, so it's important to pace yourself and know your limits. Start out with a big breakfast to keep you going through the day, or alternatively keep it light if you're heading for a pre-racing picnic. Either way, best not to start drinking too early unless you want to end up in one of those tabloid photos amid the post-racing debris. The best fun is to crack open the champers if you're lucky enough to land a big winner.

DAY TWO

Wednesday's card is often an international affair, helped in no small part by the feature event, the Prince of Wales's Stakes.

Arguably the race is first among equals of the meeting's eight Group 1s, having received significant prize-money boosts in recent years. At £750,000, it is by some way the richest purse on offer across the five days.

It is rare for the Prince of Wales's not to attract a high-calibre crop of older middle-distance horses drawn from across the racing world, with the United States, Japan and Australia all represented alongside Britain, Ireland and France in the past six years.

The Queen Mary Stakes now kicks off the action, moving up the order to take over from the Jersey Stakes. This stern test for juvenile fillies over five furlongs is the race American trainer Wesley Ward targets above all others at Royal Ascot.

The Queen's Vase slots in at second, having previously been run on the Friday. The move has been made largely to spare inexperienced three-year-olds the stress of starting next to the infield Village Enclosure, which boosts capacity at the meeting from Thursday onwards.

Last year the Vase was cut in distance from 2m to 1m6f

and upgraded from Listed to Group 2 status as part of efforts to reinforce the staying programme. Stradivarius won the first running of the race in its new guise and went on to score in the Group 1 Goodwood Cup, offering early vindication of the move, though the Vase is now somewhat in direct competition for a similar population of runners with the King Edward VII Stakes later in the meeting.

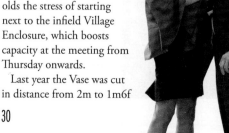

Race three is the Group 2 Duke of Cambridge Stakes, which has become a key target for trainers of older fillies and mares since its introduction in 2004. The last two editions have fallen to high-class French raiders in Usherette and Qemah, adding to the international flavour of the day.

After the Prince of Wales's Stakes the focus switches back to the straight mile and the Royal Hunt Cup, a 30-runner handicap that is one of the betting highlights of the week.

The first has become the last with the Group 3 Jersey Stakes now closing out the Wednesday action. This contest for three-year-olds over a straight seven furlongs invariably tempts connections of both sprinters and milers and last year France was successful here too, with Le Brivido.

Truly the Wednesday of Royal Ascot is a league of nations.

Wednesday June 20

2.30 Queen Mary Stakes (Group 2) *Last year's winner Heartache 5-1*	**5f** 2yo fillies	£110,000
3.05 Queen's Vase (Group 2) *Last year's winner: Stradivarius 11-2*	**1m6f** 3yo	£200,000
3.40 Duke of Cambridge Stakes (Group 2) *Last year's winner: Qemah 5-2f*	**1m** 4yo+ fillies and mares	£175,000
4.20 Prince of Wales's Stakes (Group 1) *Last year's winner: Highland Reel 9-4*	**1m2f** 4yo+	£750,000
5.00 Royal Hunt Cup (Handicap) *Last year's winner: Zhui Feng 25-1*	**1m** 3yo+	£175,000
5.35 Jersey Stakes (Group 3) *Last year's winner: Le Brivido 2-1f*	**7f** 3yo	£90,000

Race value is total prize-money

I t might seem a strange thing to say about a race run over the minimum distance of five furlongs but the Queen Mary can provide a stiff test for two-year-old fillies with relatively little racecourse experience.

Plenty come here having looked excellent prospects when winning lesser contests easily but find they have run their race before the finish.

That may help to explain why those sired by stallions who themselves had winning form at up to a mile have a decent record, with Scat Daddy, Starspangledbanner and Machiavellian all having produced winners in the past decade.

More than any of the sprint or juvenile races at the meeting, this has changed in nature since US

Key trends
► *By a sire with stamina index between 5.9f and 8.4f, 10/10*
► *Lost maiden tag, 9/10*
► *Adjusted RPR of at least 102, 9/10*
► *Rated within 9lb of RPR top-rated, 8/10*
► *Distance winner, 7/10*
► *Won last time out, 7/10*
► *Ran at least twice, 6/10*

Other factors
► *Marygate Stakes winners at York have finished 0291080; Hilary Needler 005820; National Stakes 012*
► *Two of the four winners to have had just one start were trained by Wesley Ward*

Acapulco gives
Wesley Ward a second
success in the race

phenomenon Wesley Ward began targeting Royal Ascot. Not only has the trainer won three of the last nine editions, he has compiled an extraordinary record, with his eight runners finishing 17240112, starting with Jealous Again's breakthrough success in 2009.

All of Ward's winners were well backed (as was last year's representative Happy Like A Fool, who finished second at 10-11) and most of the other recent winners were at or near the head of the market, with six of the last eight in the first three in the betting.

Away from the Ward factor, this has proved fertile ground for Irish trainers seeking to get out from the giant shadow cast by Aidan O'Brien, with Ger Lyons and Eddie Lynam among those who have scored recent successes.

Story of the last ten years

	FORM	WINNER	AGE & WGT	Adj RPR	SP	TRAINER	BEST RPR LAST 12 MONTHS (RUNS SINCE)
17	1	**Heartache** D	2 9-0	107-3	5-1	Clive Cox	won Bath Class 4 nov (5f) (0)
16	1	**Lady Aurelia**	2 9-0	112T	2-1f	Wesley Ward (USA)	won Keeneland (4½f) (0)
15	3	**Acapulco** BF	2 9-0	91-15	5-2f	Wesley Ward (USA)	3rd Churchill Downs (4½f) (0)
14	61	**Anthem Alexander** D	2 9-0	106-9	9-4f	Eddie Lynam (IRE)	won Tipperary mdn (5f) (0)
13	511	**Rizeena** CD	2 8-12	112T	6-1	Clive Brittain	won Sandown Listed (5f) (0)
12	2411	**Ceiling Kitty** D	2 8-12	106-8	20-1	Tom Dascombe	won York Listed (5f) (0)
11	11	**Best Terms** D	2 8-12	104-11	12-1	Richard Hannon snr	won Newbury Class 3 (5f) (0)
10	1	**Maqaasid** D	2 8-12	102-9	9-4f	John Gosden	won Sandown Class 4 mdn (5f) (0)
09	12	**Jealous Again** BF	2 8-12	112-7	13-2	Wesley Ward (USA)	2nd Churchill Downs Gd3 (5f) (0)
08	12	**Langs Lash** D	2 8-12	107-8	25-1	Mick Quinlan	2nd York Listed (5f) (0)

FAVOURITES £3.00

TRAINERS IN THIS RACE (w-pl-r) Wesley Ward 3-2-8, Tom Dascombe 1-0-6, Aidan O'Brien 0-0-3, Brian Meehan 0-1-2, Clive Cox 1-0-4, J S Moore 0-0-3, James Tate 0-0-2, Jeremy Noseda 0-0-2, Keith Dalgleish 0-1-4, Mark Johnston 0-0-8, Mick Channon 0-0-8, Richard Fahey 0-0-7, Richard Hannon 0-2-5, William Haggas 0-1-4, Ger Lyons 0-0-1

FATE OF FAVOURITES 0412001112 **POSITION OF WINNER IN MARKET** 0515031112

DISCOVER

Shared Racehorse Ownership

Search for your perfect ownership experience at

inthepaddock.co.uk

3.05 Queen's Vase

This 1m6f race, restricted to three-year-olds and designed to bring along future St Leger and even Cup horses over staying trips, is in its second year over that distance, having been reduced from 2m.

In its 2m incarnation the race was dominated in recent years by just four trainers and, given where the resources are spread when it comes to the best-bred middle-distance pedigrees, Mark Johnston (seven winners), Aidan O'Brien (five), Sir Michael Stoute (four) and Saeed Bin Suroor (two) are unlikely to fade from the roll of honour.

Also stocked full of the right kind of raw material is John Gosden, who had been a curious omission from the list since Landowner's 1992 victory before striking

(Run over 2m until last year)

Key trends

▶ *Top-three finish last time out, 10/10*

▶ *Adjusted RPR of at least 112, 8/10*

▶ *Rated within 3lb of RPR top-rated, 8/10*

▶ *Recorded a pre-race RPR of at least 99, 8/10*

▶ *By a sire with a stamina index in excess of 1m2f, 8/10*

▶ *Won that season, 6/10*

Other factors

▶ *Estimate in 2012 was the only winner to come straight from maiden company*

▶ *Five winners contested a Listed or Group race last time out*

12 months ago with Stradivarius.

Despite the elevation of the Vase from Listed to Group 2 status, Stradivarius

came via the handicap route in 2017, though his runner-up effort at Chester prior to Ascot had earned him an RPR of 100.

That sample of one bears out the data from previous years, with a minimum Racing Post Rating of 98 featuring in the records of 15 of the last 20 winners.

It is difficult to know how the trends might change at the shorter distance but, even when the race was run over 2m, several winners had been campaigned as Derby prospects.

The 2007 winner Mahler actually ran at Epsom, finishing 11th to Authorized, while in the past 20 years three Vase victors took in the Lingfield Derby Trial and one each came via the Cocked Hat Stakes at Goodwood and the Ballysax Stakes at Leopardstown.

Story of the last ten years

	FORM	WINNER		AGE & WGT	Adj RPR	SP	TRAINER	BEST RPR LAST 12 MONTHS (RUNS SINCE)
17	41-12	**Stradivarius** BF	3	9-0	114-3	11-2	John Gosden	2nd Chester Class 3 hcap (1m4½f) (0)
16	3-213	**Sword Fighter**	3	9-3	99-16	33-1	Aidan O'Brien (IRE)	3rd Naas (1m4f) (0)
15	212-	**Aloft**	3	9-3	123T	5-2f	Aidan O'Brien (IRE)	2nd Racing Post Trophy Gp1 (1m) (0)
14	13-52	**Hartnell**	3	9-3	115T	7-2	Mark Johnston	2nd Lingfield Derby Trial Listed (1m3½f) (0)
13	41-11	**Leading Light**	3	9-4	121-T	5-4f	Aidan O'Brien (IRE)	won Gallinule Stakes Gp3 (1m2f) (0)
12	7-1	**Estimate**	3	8-12	98-21	3-1f	Sir Michael Stoute	won Salisbury Class 5 mdn (1m4f) (0)
11	45243	**Namibian**	3	9-1	121-T	7-2f	Mark Johnston	3rd Musselburgh Class 2 hcap (1m4½f) (0)
10	612-3	**Mikhail Glinka** BF	3	9-1	120-2	2-1f	Aidan O'Brien (IRE)	2nd Criterium de Saint-Cloud Gp1 (1m2f) (1)
09	11-13	**Holberg**	3	9-1	112-3	7-1	Mark Johnston	3rd Glasgow Stakes Listed (1m3f) (0)
08	1-321	**Patkai**	3	9-1	122T	6-4f	Sir Michael Stoute	won Haydock Class 2 hcap (1m4f) (0)

FAVOURITES £9.75

TRAINERS IN THIS RACE (w-pl-r) Aidan O'Brien 4-3-15, Mark Johnston 3-1-17, John Gosden 1-2-6, Andrew Balding 0-1-7, Charlie Appleby 0-1-3, Dermot Weld 0-0-3, David Elsworth 0-0-3, David Simcock 0-0-2

FATE OF FAVOURITES 1011113144 **POSITION OF WINNER IN MARKET** 1311112102

Unlike the mile Group 1 for three-year-old fillies, Friday's Coronation Stakes, this Group 2 contest for older fillies and mares is run over the straight mile.

If there is one striking statistic that leaps off the pages during the relatively short history of this race, it is the appalling record of those who have had to carry a Group 1 penalty. In the 14 editions to date, ten horses have lined up under a penalty and all were beaten, with only Soviet Song in 2005 making the frame.

Part of the explanation for such a poor record among those asked to concede weight all round might be the race's role as a launch pad for the season, as four of those ten with a Group 1 penalty had not had a previous run that year.

That contrasts starkly with the profile of the 14 winners, all but one of whom had run at least once that season.

It should be noted that the Group 1 penalty only applies to wins after August 31 the previous season and so having winning form at that level does not preclude a big performance here, as was demonstrated by the 2017 heroine Qemah, who had won the Coronation Stakes and Prix Rothschild in the summer of 2016.

The Princess Elizabeth Stakes at Epsom has proved a useful stepping stone, with four of the 14 winning fillies having used that as a warm-up, though curiously none of them were successful there.

Key trends

▸ *Top-three finish that season,* *10/10*
▸ *Had won a Group race,* *10/10*
▸ *Adjusted RPR of at least 125,* *9/10*
▸ *Rated within 6lb of RPR top-rated, 9/10*
▸ *Distance winner, 7/10*

Other factors

▸ *Winners of the Dahlia at Newmarket finished 22153941; Chartwell at Lingfield 1020*
▸ *Three had already won at Ascot and one was Group-placed at the previous year's Royal Ascot*

Strawberrydaiquiri (right) battles to victory in 2010

Story of the last ten years

	FORM	WINNER	AGE & WGT	Adj RPR	SP	TRAINER	BEST RPR LAST 12 MONTHS (RUNS SINCE)
17	113-2	**Qemah** C, D	4 9-0	131^T	5-2f	Jean-Claude Rouget (FR)	won Prix Rothschild Gp1 (1m) (2)
16	7-111	**Usherette** D	4 9-3	128^{-1}	9-4f	Andre Fabre (FR)	won Dahlia Stakes Gp2 (1m1f) (0)
15	00-33	**Amazing Maria**	4 9-0	119^{-9}	25-1	David O'Meara	3rd Lanwades Stud Stakes Gp2 (1m) (0)
14	712-2	**Integral** D, BF	4 9-0	130^T	9-4f	Sir Michael Stoute	2nd Sun Chariot Stakes Gp1 (1m) (1)
13	11d-1	**Duntle** CD	4 8-12	131^{-1}	10-3	David Wachman (IRE)	2nd Matron Stakes Gp1 (1m) (1)
12	647-2	**Joviality**	4 8-12	125^{-6}	11-1	John Gosden	4th Falmouth Stakes Gp1 (1m) (2)
11	-1122	**Lolly For Dolly** D, BF	4 8-12	127^{-4}	11-1	Tommy Stack (IRE)	won Gladness Stakes Gp3 (7f) (2)
10	114-1	**Strawberrydaiquiri** C, D	4 8-12	132^T	9-2	Sir Michael Stoute	won Sandown Listed (1m) (2)
09	144-3	**Spacious** D, BF	4 8-12	125^{-6}	10-1	James Fanshawe	4th Coronation Stakes Gp1 (1m) (4)
08	931-1	**Sabana Perdida**	5 8-12	129^{-2}	4-1	Alain de Royer-Dupre (FR)	won Chartwell Fillies' Stakes Gp3 (7f) (0)

WINS-PL-RUNS 4yo 9-10-85, 5yo 1-8-27, 6yo+ 0-1-3 **FAVOURITES** £0.00

TRAINERS IN THIS RACE (w-pl-r) John Gosden 1-1-5, Sir Michael Stoute 2-3-9, Andre Fabre 1-1-4, Aidan O'Brien 0-0-1, Jim Bolger 0-0-3, Graham Motion 0-0-1, Ed Dunlop 0-0-3, Roger Varian 0-0-5, Mick Channon 0-1-7

FATE OF FAVOURITES 2634061511 **POSITION OF WINNER IN MARKET** 2525521511

Register your yearling for Plus 10

+ More than **£13 million** in bonus Prize money has been paid out to date

+ Rewarding almost **700 individual breeders**

+ **Breeders win up to £2,000** if their horse wins a Plus 10 race

📅 **Yearling registration** of **£200** is due by **30 June.**

www.plus10bonus.com

+44 (0) 20 7152 0026

⁺10
PLUS TEN

⁺10 141

This is one of the highlights of the European season at a mile and a quarter and also one of the last chances for the cream of the older middle-distance crop to race one another on level terms before having to face the three-year-olds and their weight-for-age allowance.

The typical winner has already proved top class, both in terms of races won and ratings achieved, with an adjusted RPR of 136 applicable to all but one of the last ten winners.

The 2017 winner Highland Reel certainly ticked both boxes, having scored five times previously at Group or Grade 1 level, though in at least one sense he might be regarded as a slight outlier, given that all of those, bar his breakthrough success in the Secretariat Stakes at Arlington, were at a mile and a half.

More broadly it is a race that tends to fall to those who have already won at Group 1 level. Since the Prince of Wales's Stakes was promoted to the top rank in 2000, only three of the 18 winners were scoring a maiden success in that grade.

Whether that particular trend might be on the wane is open to question but it should be noted that the trio of first-time Group 1

Story of the last ten years

	FORM	WINNER	AGE	& WGT	Adj RPR	SP	TRAINER	BEST RPR LAST 12 MONTHS (RUNS SINCE)
17	12-71	**Highland Reel** C, D	5	9-0	138-1	9-4	Aidan O'Brien (IRE)	2nd Prix de l'Arc de Triomphe Gp1 (1m4f) (4)
16	11-15	**My Dream Boat** D	4	9-0	134-11	16-1	Clive Cox	won Gordon Richards Stakes Gp3 (1m2f) (1)
15	2/13-	**Free Eagle** D	4	9-0	136-4	5-2f	Dermot Weld (IRE)	3rd Champion Stakes Gp1 (1m2f) (0)
14	122-0	**The Fugue** D	5	8-11	140-8	11-2	John Gosden	won Irish Champion Stakes Gp1 (1m2f) (3)
13	/1-11	**Al Kazeem** D	5	9-0	137T	11-4	Roger Charlton	won Tattersalls Gold Cup Gp1 (1m2½f) (0)
12	26-41	**So You Think** D	6	9-0	142T	4-5f	Aidan O'Brien (IRE)	won Eclipse Stakes Gp1 (1m2f) (6)
11	316-1	**Rewilding**	4	9-0	138-5	17-2	Mahmood Al Zarooni	won Dubai Sheema Classic Gp1 (1m4f) (0)
10	4-112	**Byword**	4	9-0	139T	5-2f	Andre Fabre (FR)	2nd Prix d'Ispahan Gp1 (1m1f) (0)
09	15-31	**Vision D'Etat** D	4	9-0	138-1	4-1	Eric Libaud (FR)	5th Prix de l'Arc de Triomphe Gp1 (1m4f) (2)
08	23-11	**Duke Of Marmalade** D	4	9-0	140T	Evsf	Aidan O'Brien (IRE)	won Tattersalls Gold Cup (1m2½f) (0)

WINS-PL-RUNS 4yo 6-14-50, 5yo 3-3-29, 6yo+ 1-1-13 **FAVOURITES** £0.80

TRAINERS IN THIS RACE (w-pl-r) Aidan O'Brien 3-3-12, Clive Cox 1-0-1, Dermot Weld 1-0-1, John Gosden 1-4-11, Roger Charlton 1-1-2, Charlie Appleby 0-0-2, Jim Bolger 0-0-1, Jean-Claude Rouget 0-1-2, Roger Varian 0-0-3, Saeed Bin Suroor 0-1-4, Sir Michael Stoute 0-3-8, William Haggas 0-1-2

FATE OF FAVOURITES 1212143168 **POSITION OF WINNER IN MARKET** 1313122162

winners – Byword, Free Eagle and My Dream Boat – have all struck in the last eight editions.

In terms of prep races that have a strong influence on the outcome, Britain is late in staging its first Group 1 of the season over the trip in comparison to Ireland and France, which means there have been a wide variety of successful routes.

While a pair of trials at Sandown – the Group 3 Gordon Richards Stakes and the Group 2 Brigadier Gerard Stakes – are often cited as useful pointers, this contest requires a further step up.

Since 2000 all 16 winners who had already raced that season had posted their most recent outing at Group 1 level (though Al Kazeem in 2013 and My Dream Boat in 2016 both won at Sandown earlier in their campaigns).

The Tattersalls Gold Cup has been the chosen warm-up for five winners during that period (among that number only Azamour in 2005 was beaten at the Curragh), while France's two early-season Group 1s, the Prix d'Ispahan and the Prix Ganay, account for three winners between them.

One factor that shouldn't put punters off is a horse who comes to Ascot off a break after having run on Dubai World Cup night at the end of March.

The 2014 heroine The Fugue is the most recent of four Prince of Wales's winners this century who were having their first European start since returning from the Middle East.

Highland Reel (left) and Free Eagle (right) won either side of My Dream Boat, trained by Clive Cox (above)

Key trends

▶ *Adjusted RPR of at least 136, 9/10*
▶ *Rated within 8lb of RPR top-rated, 9/10 (four winners were top-rated)*
▶ *Aged four or five, 9/10*
▶ *Distance winner, 7/10*
▶ *Previous Group 1 winner, 7/10*
▶ *Between seven and 17 career runs, 6/10*

Other factors

▶ *Seven fillies have gone to post, finishing 8313524*
▶ *The record of Gordon Richards winners is 52681313*
▶ *In 2015 Free Eagle became the first horse to take this on his seasonal reappearance since Rakti in 2004*

PRINCE OF WALES'S STAKES

LEGENDARY WINNERS

Hyperion (1933)

One of the best Derby winners of the 20th century and his unbeaten Classic season also included victories in the St Leger and the Prince of Wales's Stakes, which at that time was open to three-year-olds; left an even greater mark at stud and was champion sire six times

Dubai Millennium

Dubai Millennium (2000)

One of the modern-day greats on dirt and turf; won the Dubai World Cup on dirt by six lengths before an eight-length Prince of Wales's Stakes victory on turf at Royal Ascot; sadly that was his final run and he died the following year

BETTING

Longest-priced winner: Bob Back 33-1 (1985)

Shortest-priced winner: Royal Palace 1-4 (1968)

Market leaders: 21 favourites or joint favourites have been successful in 50 runnings

DID YOU KNOW?

King George VI

When racing resumed at Royal Ascot in 1946 after the war, there was no Prince of Wales's Stakes because George VI was on the throne and, as he had no male heirs, there was no Prince of Wales. The race did not take place again until 1968, a year before the current Prince of Wales's investiture

WINNING CONNECTIONS

Most successful trainer
5 wins: Sir Henry Cecil
Lucky Wednesday (1977)
Gunner B (1978)
Perpendicular (1992)
Placerville (1993)
Bosra Sham (1997)

Most successful jockey
5 wins: Pat Eddery
Record Run (1975)
English Spring (1986)
Two Timing (1989)
Batshoof (1990)
Placerville (1993)

Most successful owner
5 wins: Godolphin
Faithful Son (1998)
Dubai Millennium (2000)
Fantastic Light (2001)
Grandera (2002)
Rewilding (2011)

All figures since 1968

This 30-runner handicap over the straight mile has a reputation as one of the biggest betting heats of the week, though figures from Coral suggest that, by turnover at least, it has not ranked higher than eighth among the 30 races at the meeting in any of the last three years.

One constant is that this remains a race where extreme weight-carrying performances are difficult to achieve. Going back to the reopening of Ascot and its newly relaid track in 2006, no winner has been rated within 5lb of the topweight, while only two winners have carried in excess of 9st 3lb.

Those at the top of the handicap can run well – seven horses carrying 9st 6lb or more have been placed in the past decade – but the last winner to defy such a weight was Governorship in 1988.

Key trends

▶ *Recorded a pre-race RPR of at least 99, 10/10*
▶ *Officially rated between 93 and 103, 9/10 (exception was penalised)*
▶ *Rated within 7lb of RPR top-rated, 9/10*
▶ *Won or placed in a field of at least 14 runners, 9/10*
▶ *Top-four finish at least once that season, 9/10 (exception was making seasonal debut)*
▶ *Carried between 8st 8lb and 9st 3lb, 8/10 (both exceptions carried 9st 5lb)*
▶ *Distance winner, 8/10*

With only two winners having had a single-figure number cloth (both wore eight) and the lowest-rated being number 22 on the racecard over the 12 editions run at the new Ascot, the middle of the weights would appear to be the optimum.

Where that sweet spot falls in terms of official ratings

has varied quite considerably, with 93 the basement and 105 the second highest (2008 winner Mr Aviator was rated 110, though he still had seven horses above him in the handicap).

As might be expected in such a race, the market has been no better than a fair guide, though half the winners since 2006 were returned at 16-1 or shorter. The record of 'plunge' horses has not been great, though admittedly from a small sample.

Backers of Abseil at 7-2 in 2014 and Dimension at 9-2 (2012) were left empty-handed, while 13-8 hotpot Bankable was arguably undone by a draw bias that heavily favoured high-numbered stalls when finishing fifth in 2008.

Against those examples, Forgotten Voice went off the 4-1 favourite in 2009 and duly obliged by daylight.

Story of the last ten years

	FORM	WINNER		AGE & WGT	OR	SP	TRAINER	BEST RPR LAST 12 MONTHS (RUNS SINCE)
17	-4803	**Zhui Feng**		4 9-0	100-3	25-1	Amanda Perrett	4th Winter Derby Gp3 (1m2f) (3)
16	125-1	**Portage** (5ex) CD		4 9-5	105-7	10-1	Mick Halford (IRE)	5th Newmarket Class 2 hcap (1m1f) (1)
15	43-02	**Gm Hopkins** D, BF		4 9-3	103-2	8-1	John Gosden	2nd Newbury Class 2 hcap (1m) (0)
14	5950-	**Field Of Dream** C		7 9-1	101-1	20-1	Jamie Osborne	won Newmarket Class 2 hcap (7f) (4)
13	-0020	**Belgian Bill** D		5 8-11	97-2	33-1	George Baker	won Kempton Class 2 hcap (7f) (6)
12	541-2	**Prince Of Johanne** D		6 9-3	100-1	16-1	Tom Tate	2nd York Listed hcap (1m) (0)
11	10-33	**Julienas** D, BF		4 8-8	93-2	12-1	Walter Swinburn	3rd Sandown Class 3 hcap (1m) (0)
10	19-44	**Invisible Man** D		4 8-9	95-7	28-1	Saeed Bin Suroor	won Pontefract Class 3 hcap (1m) (3)
09	1/11	**Forgotten Voice** D		4 9-1	101-3	4-1f	Jeremy Noseda	won Kempton Class 3 hcap (1m) (0)
08	12120	**Mr Aviator** D		4 9-5	102-13	25-1	Richard Hannon snr	2nd Lingfield Class 2 hcap (1m2f) (1)

WINS-PL-RUNS 4yo 7-13-116, 5yo 1-10-78, 6yo+ 2-7-90 **FAVOURITES** -£8.20

FATE OF FAVOURITES 5102000000 **POSITION OF WINNER IN MARKET** 8104608230

Summer in the city

The distance of seven furlongs for this Group 3 race makes it something of a battleground between Classic pretenders dropping back from a mile and sprinters trying to stretch out their stamina.

The trend in recent years has been for those who have run in a Guineas to hold sway, with seven of the last ten winners having run in at least one in Britain, Ireland or France, compared to just two in the previous decade.

That emphasis on having been highly tried is also evident in looking at the two-year-old records of past winners. Given where Ascot falls in the calendar it is no surprise that 18 of the last 20 winners raced at two but perhaps more telling is the fact that, among them, 13

Key trends

▶ *Adjusted Racing Post Rating of at least 118, 10/10*
▶ *First or second in one or both of last two starts, 9/10*
▶ *Rated within 9lb of RPR top-rated, 9/10*
▶ *Distance winner, 7/10*
▶ *Won as a three-year-old, 7/10*
▶ *Top-three finish last time out, 7/10*

Other factors

▶ *Fillies don't have a great record overall, but they won in 2010 and 2012 (Rainfall and Ishvana)*
▶ *Winners of the King Charles II at Newmarket have finished 95237420*
▶ *Seven of the last ten winners had run in a Guineas*
▶ *Five winners had run in Classic trials but only one was successful*

had a first-four finish to their name at Group level during their juvenile season.

That need to have performed to a high level is further illustrated by the peak RPRs of winners heading into the race, with 16 of the last 20 winners having previously run to an RPR of 106+.

Last year Le Brivido had run to a Racing Post Rating of 118 in narrowly losing out in the Poule d'Essai des Poulains, the highest since Diktat scored in 1998.

Perhaps it is a function of trends in breeding but 13 of the last 20 winners were by sires with a stamina index in the relatively narrow range between 7.6 and 8.6 furlongs, a score that rises to eight out of ten when concentrating on the past decade.

Story of the last ten years

	FORM	WINNER	AGE & WGT	Adj RPR	SP	TRAINER	BEST RPR LAST 12 MONTHS (RUNS SINCE)
17	1-12	**Le Brivido**	3 9-1	131^T	2-1f	Andre Fabre (FR)	2nd Poule d'Essai des Poulains Gp1 (1m) (0)
16	1-2d3	**Ribchester**	3 9-6	122$^{.5}$	7-1	Richard Fahey	won Mill Reef Stakes Gp2 (6f) (2)
15	113-7	**Dutch Connection** D	3 9-4	118$^{.9}$	14-1	Charlie Hills	3rd National Stakes Gp1 (7f) (1)
14	12-13	**Mustajeeb** D	3 9-4	124$^{.4}$	9-2j	Dermot Weld (IRE)	won Amethyst Stakes Gp3 (1m) (1)
13	3-142	**Gale Force Ten** D	3 9-1	128^T	9-2f	Aidan O'Brien (IRE)	2nd Irish 2,000 Guineas Gp1 (1m) (0)
12	29132	**Ishvana** D	3 8-12	125$^{.2}$	20-1	Aidan O'Brien (IRE)	2nd Irish 2,000 Guineas Gp1 (1m) (0)
11	132-6	**Strong Suit** C	3 9-6	122$^{.6}$	11-1	Richard Hannon snr	won Coventry Stakes Gp2 (6f) (3)
10	12	**Rainfall** D	3 8-12	122$^{.5}$	8-1	Mark Johnston	2nd Haydock Listed (6f) (0)
09	19-10	**Ouqba** D	3 9-1	126$^{.2}$	12-1	Barry Hills	won Free Handicap (7f) (1)
08	3-1	**Aqlaam** D	3 9-1	118$^{.10}$	13-2	William Haggas	won Newbury Class 4 mdn (7f) (0)

FAVOURITES £1.25

TRAINERS IN THIS RACE (w-pl-r) Aidan O'Brien 2-2-14, Mark Johnston 1-0-4, William Haggas 1-2-8, Charlie Hills 1-0-7, Andrew Balding 0-1-4, Brian Meehan 0-0-4, David Elsworth 0-0-2, Hugo Palmer 0-0-2, Jeremy Noseda 0-1-7, John Gosden 0-1-10, Marco Botti 0-0-1, Roger Varian 0-1-4, Saeed Bin Suroor 0-3-9, Sir Michael Stoute 0-2-3

FATE OF FAVOURITES 0062311061 **POSITION OF WINNER IN MARKET** 2755811621

BIG GUNS RULE IN THE TOP RACES

Five of the eight Group 1 races were shared between Ballydoyle and Godolphin and the powerhouse operations were also responsible for the runner-up in two that went by the wayside. In the St James's Palace Stakes won by Barney Roy, they were responsible for five of the eight runners between them, while in the Coronation Stakes Aidan O'Brien saddled the 1-2-3 from as many runners. With the power battle so important to both operations, their famous colours are sure to be the fore again.

DON'T IGNORE SMALLER YARDS

A fast two-year-old can be the breakthrough horse for a smaller or up-and-coming trainer and it proved to be the case again last year for Richard Spencer with Rajasinghe *(above and right)* in the Coventry Stakes and French trainer Matthieu Palussiere with Different League in the Albany Stakes. Those winners struck at 11-1 and 20-1, emphasising that lesser-known trainers should not be ignored in the juvenile contests. Eight trainers in the past decade have had their first Royal Ascot winner with a two-year-old.

Lessons from last year

FOREIGN RAIDERS OFTEN DO WELL

Each year Ascot's international recruitment drive continues to bear more fruit. Five races went to raiders from outside Britain and Ireland in 2017, four of them on the first two days. French trainers took three of those and they look set to mount another strong challenge, with last year's Jersey Stakes winner Le Brivido *(below)* a leading fancy to open the 2018 meeting with a bang in the Queen Anne Stakes.

HOME SPRINTERS ARE ON THE UP

Lady Aurelia became the first international winner of the King's Stand Stakes since 2012 (and her trainer Wesley Ward also sent out the last foreign raider to land the Diamond Jubilee Stakes in 2015) but last year was also notable for the continued resurgence of domestic sprinting. Track specialist The Tin Man led home a British 1-2-3 in the Diamond Jubilee, making it four wins in the last five for the British and Irish sprinters in both that race and the King's Stand.

LOOK BEYOND FAVOURITES

Seven favourites were successful, although three of the five odds-on chances were turned over and favourites drew a blank on Gold Cup day. Of the 34 horses sent off second best in the betting, 11 won, resulting in an excellent level-stakes profit of +27.25pt. The best races for favourites in the past decade have been the St James's Palace Stakes (seven winners), Gold Cup (six) and Queen's Vase (six). Outsiders have done best in the past decade in the Windsor Castle Stakes (six winners outside the top six in the betting) and the Royal Hunt Cup (five).

FIVE OF THE BEST . . .

TAKE A HAMPER

Picnics, whether in the car park or the Windsor Enclosure, are one of the special delights of Royal Ascot, especially if the week brings glorious summer weather. You can pre-order from the racecourse or create your own, but be sure to check out the picnic policy (see page 6). Cucumber sandwiches, strawberries and cream and a bottle of fizz are perennial favourites to make it a day to remember.

DRESS UP

Royal Ascot is the perfect excuse to shed your usual weekday skin and show off your sartorial prowess.

A good way to think of the occasion is to dress as if you're attending a family wedding – and then add a little more flair on top. That doesn't necessarily mean a top hat and tails for the men, unless you're in the Royal Enclosure, but for ladies a hat is always a good idea. And a splash of summer colour always goes down well.

GRAB A RINGSIDE SEAT

One of the best places to see the royal procession up close each day is the parade ring, where the Queen and her guests arrive in a grand circle shortly after 2pm once they have turned off the racecourse. This is the signal that racing is about to start and the runners for the first race are quickly on parade, adding to the buzz. Get there early to make sure you're in prime position as the crowds soon build up.

STAND BY THE RAILS

Many will grab a place by the rails for the royal procession, but being there as the sporting action unfolds on the track is something else. With the roar of the crowd and the thunder of hooves, a spot by the rails takes you into an auditorium of crackling excitement and, even if your horse doesn't place, you'll experience a unique kind of euphoria. The nearer you can get to the winning post the better.

SING ALONG

What do Brits love more than a good sing-song? Every day at Royal Ascot is rounded off with a session of communal singing at the bandstand, a tradition that has been going since the 1970s. The hymn sheet goes from patriotic ballads such as Land of Hope and Glory to modern classics like Neil Diamond's Sweet Caroline. Don't worry if you're not sure of the words, they're displayed on a big screen – and nobody cares much anyway.

DAY THREE

*S*tyle takes centre stage in the enclosures on Ladies' Day, while the main attraction out on the track is the Gold Cup, which was first run in 1807 and is not only the oldest race of the week but also one of the most prestigious.

The Gold Cup, run over a distance of two miles, three furlongs and 210 yards, comes down to survival of the fittest and is a test of courage and class in equal measure. Only the special ones succeed.

Victory in 2017 went to Big Orange as he somehow managed to withstand the late surge of defending champion Order Of St George to give trainer Michael Bell and jockey James Doyle a first success in one of the most famous Flat races in the calendar.

That was proof, if it were needed, that Ascot's staying races can be just as thrilling as the helter-skelter of the sprints.

The day starts at the other end of the spectrum with speedy juveniles scorching the turf in the Norfolk Stakes over the minimum trip of five furlongs.

The other four races are all restricted to three-year-olds and the first of them is the Group 3 Hampton Court Stakes, followed by the Group 2 Ribblesdale Stakes for fillies – a fitting contest for Ladies' Day. If the King Edward VII Stakes on the Friday is the Ascot Derby, the Ribblesdale is the Ascot Oaks and is often contested by fillies who have been on the Classic trail in the spring.

After the Gold Cup, the day closes with a pair of fiercely contested handicaps for three-year-olds – the Britannia over a mile and the 1m4f King George V, which is often an early pointer to Gold Cup contenders of the future.

From the enclosures to the track, Thursday is a showcase for the infinite variety of Royal Ascot. Long may it reign.

RUNNING ORDER

2.30 Norfolk Stakes (Group 2) *Last year's winner: Sioux Nation 14-1*	**5f** 2yo	£100,000
3.05 Hampton Court Stakes (Group 3) *Last year's winner: Benbatl 9-2*	**1m2f** 3yo	£90,000
3.40 Ribblesdale Stakes (Group 2) *Last year's winner: Coronet 9-1*	**1m4f** 3yo fillies	£200,000
4.20 Gold Cup (Group 1) *Last year's winner: Big Orange 5-1*	**2m4f** 4yo+	£500,000
5.00 Britannia Stakes (Handicap) *Last year's winner: Bless Him 25-1*	**1m** 3yo colts and geldings	£120,000
5.35 King George V Stakes (Handicap) *Last year's winner: Atty Persse 7-1*	**1m4f** 3yo	£90,000

Race value is total prize-money

2.30 Norfolk Stakes

This is the meeting's third Group 2 race for two-year-olds, following the Coventry and Queen Mary Stakes, and its distinguishing feature is that it is open to both sexes over the minimum distance of five furlongs.

Possibly because of the race distance, the Norfolk has a mixed record of producing enduring stars with six of the last ten winners failing to notch another victory that year but three of the other four going on to Group 1 success (and the fourth taking the Group 2 Gimcrack).

As this is often the major target for a speedy and precocious two-year-old, it is no surprise to find that most winners have been pushed hard enough beforehand to achieve an adjusted RPR well

into three figures and you have to go all the way back to 1990 to find the last maiden who scored a first win here.

The extent to which connections know what they have on their hands is clear from the winning odds, with only three of the last 20 winners going off bigger than 10-1. Five of the 20 were favourite, with another ten being second or third in the betting.

Nine of the last 20 winners had won their only start, with connections happy they had done enough before Ascot (two others were unbeaten in two or three starts).

It is almost essential to come here off the back of a victory, with 18 of the last 20 winners having done so (the two exceptions had been unplaced in Listed races).

Along with the ever-dangerous Aidan O'Brien, trainers known for fast horses have done well, including Wesley Ward, Richard Hannon, William Haggas, Clive Cox, Kevin Ryan and Robert Cowell. Another trainer to note is Mark Johnston, who won in 2003 and has had a second, third and fourth in the last three runnings.

Key trends
▶ *Lost maiden tag, 10/10*
▶ *By a sire with a stamina index between 6.7f and 8.3f, 10/10*
▶ *Adjusted RPR of at least 103, 9/10*
▶ *Won last time out, 8/10*
▶ *Won most recent start by at least two lengths, 6/10*

Other factors
▶ *Five were once-raced winners. The other five were all beaten on their debut*

Story of the last ten years

	FORM	WINNER	AGE & WGT	Adj RPR	SP	TRAINER	BEST RPR LAST 12 MONTHS (RUNS SINCE)
17	3216	**Sioux Nation**	2 9-1	103-10	14-1	Aidan O'Brien (IRE)	won Cork mdn (6f) (1)
16	1	**Prince Lir** D	2 9-1	105-11	8-1	Robert Cowell	won Beverley Class 2 (5f) (0)
15	6321	**Waterloo Bridge** D	2 9-1	97-23	12-1	Aidan O'Brien (IRE)	won Tipperary mdn (5f) (0)
14	211	**Baitha Alga**	2 9-1	110-2	9-1	Richard Hannon	won Woodcote Stakes Listed (6f) (0)
13	1	**No Nay Never**	2 9-1	104-10	4-1	Wesley Ward (USA)	won Keeneland (4½f) (0)
12	1	**Reckless Abandon** D	2 9-1	107-6	4-1	Clive Cox	won Doncaster Class 5 mdn auct (5f) (0)
11	1	**Bapak Chinta** D	2 9-1	107-6	6-1	Kevin Ryan	won Hamilton Class 5 mdn (5f) (0)
10	314	**Approve** D	2 9-1	104-7	16-1	William Haggas	4th Woodcote Stakes Listed (6f) (0)
09	21	**Radiohead** D	2 9-1	105-14	10-1	Brian Meehan	won Bath Class 5 mdn (5f) (0)
08	1	**South Central** D	2 9-1	115T	11-4f	Howard Johnson	won Carlisle Class 6 mdn auct (5f) (0)

FAVOURITES -£6.25

TRAINERS IN THIS RACE (w-pl-r): Aidan O'Brien 2-2-7, Clive Cox 1-0-2, Richard Hannon 1-2-5, Wesley Ward 1-0-6, Charlie Hills 0-0-1, Peter Chapple-Hyam 0-1-4, James Given 0-0-4, Karl Burke 0-1-2, Mark Johnston 0-2-10, Richard Fahey 0-0-3, Tom Dascombe 0-0-4

FATE OF FAVOURITES 1560625352 **POSITION OF WINNER IN MARKET** 1463223359

This Group 3 race for three-year-olds, which was added to the programme when Royal Ascot was extended to five days in 2002 and upgraded to its current level in 2011, can showcase an up-and-coming star with three of the last four winners going on to Group 1 success – Hawkbill *(pictured)* did so on his very next start in the Coral-Eclipse in 2016 – and the other one of that quartet, Time Test, also developing into a Group 1 performer as well as a Group 2 winner.

The roll of honour is dominated by the big yards that house plenty of later-developing three-year-olds, with seven of the last ten winners having come from Newmarket and further back the 2004 and 2005 winners having been trained by Aidan O'Brien (more

Key trends
▶ *Yet to win at this level or higher, 10/10*
▶ *Adjusted RPR of at least 117, 10/10*
▶ *Rated within 6lb of RPR top-rated, 9/10*
▶ *Top-four finish last time out, 7/10 (two exceptions beaten in the Derby)*
▶ *Won that season, 7/10*
▶ *Distance winner, 6/10*

Other factors
▶ *Four had won a handicap that season*
▶ *Four had been beaten in Classic trials, including three who finished 632 in the Dante*

recently he had the second and fourth last year and the third in 2016).

There are two main routes to this race – either through handicaps (three of the last five winners) or from the Classic trail (Energizer in 2012 and Benbatl last year had finished just outside the places in Classics).

Most winners had done enough to take high rank in the betting, with six of the last ten coming from the top two and only one of the ten priced at bigger than 8-1.

Five of the 16 winners since 2002 were unraced as two-year-olds but most of the others had won at that age and a last-time-out success is a good pointer, although failure to win can be excused if that run was in a Classic or another Group 1.

Story of the last ten years

	FORM	WINNER	AGE & WGT	Adj RPR	SP	TRAINER	BEST RPR LAST 12 MONTHS (RUNS SINCE)
17	1325	**Benbatl**	3 9-0	128T	9-2	Saeed Bin Suroor	5th Derby Gp1 (1m4f) (0)
16	111-1	**Hawkbill** D	3 9-0	121-4	11-2	Charlie Appleby	won Newmarket Listed (1m2f) (0)
15	212-1	**Time Test** D	3 9-0	123T	15-8f	Roger Charlton	won Newbury Class 2 hcap (1m2f) (0)
14	2-11	**Cannock Chase** D	3 9-0	122-1	7-4f	Sir Michael Stoute	won Newbury Class 2 hcap (1m2f) (0)
13	311	**Remote** D	3 9-0	127T	9-4f	John Gosden	won Doncaster Class 2 hcap (1m) (0
12	45-24	**Energizer**	3 9-0	122T	15-2	Jens Hirschberger (GER)	4th Cologne Gp2 (1m) (0)
11	28-39	**Pisco Sour**	3 9-0	121-2	20-1	Hughie Morrison	3rd Dante Stakes Gp2 (1m2½f) (1)
10	211	**Afsare** D	3 9-5	117-12	9-4f	Luca Cumani	won Doncaster Class 2 (1m2f) (0)
09	71-56	**Glass Harmonium**	3 9-2	123-4	8-1	Sir Michael Stoute	6th Dante Stakes Gp2 (1m2½f) (0)
08	21-61	**Collection** D	3 9-2	117-6	13-2	William Haggas	won York Class 4 hcap (1m2½f) (0)

FAVOURITES £2.13

TRAINERS IN THIS RACE (w-pl-r) Sir Michael Stoute 2-1-10, Charlie Appleby 1-0-2, Saeed Bin Suroor 1-1-8, Aidan O'Brien 0-3-9, Andrew Balding 0-0-3, Richard Hannon 0-1-3

FATE OF FAVOURITES 0510011122 **POSITION OF WINNER IN MARKET** 2410611142

Injured Jockeys Fund

Peter O'Sullevan House

The Injured Jockeys Fund's third Rehabilitation and Fitness Centre is being built in Newmarket. The centre will complement the IJF's two other centres Oaksey House in Lambourn and Jack Berry House in Malton.

Opening in 2019 the centre will be situated alongside the British Racing School. Offering state-of-the-art facilities to licence holders in the UK and the local racing community. We are very grateful to our supporters and to the many people who kindly donate and help us to continue our work to educate and care for our sports men and women.

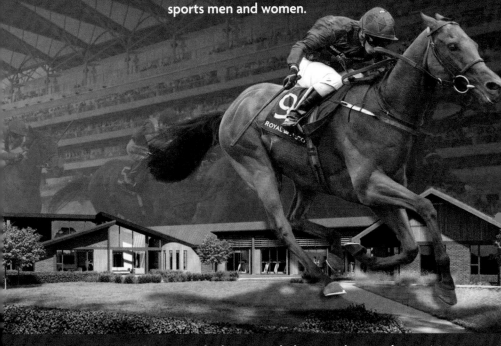

To find out more and ways in which you can help or to donate please visit:

www.ijf.org.uk or telephone: 01638 662 246

This is the meeting's premier race for middle-distance filles from the Classic generation and often draws runners who have competed in the Oaks or at least the trials.

Five of the last ten winners had run in a Guineas or the Oaks, although none finished closer than fifth and that explains why they were going for this Group 2 rather than a top-level target.

To a large extent this race draws still-developing fillies, with seven of the last ten winners having run no more than four times before this assignment (two of the exceptions came from Irish stables), but most of them had shown enough ability to be tried in Pattern company.

The top level might be beyond them at this stage but if you remove Group 1

DID YOU KNOW?

Royal Ascot is Britain's most popular race meeting, welcoming 300,000 racegoers across five days, with 173,000 racecards printed

Key trends

▶ *Raced no more than three times at two, 9/10*
▶ *Adjusted RPR of at least 113, 9/10*
▶ *Contested a Listed or Group race, 9/10 (six had won a Group race)*
▶ *Won one of last two starts, 8/10*
▶ *Won over at least 1m2f, 7/10*

Other factors

▶ *Three winners were RPR top-rated, but five of the other seven were between 7lb and 16lb off top*
▶ *Two winners failed to win the previous season, while two did not run as juveniles*
▶ *Six winners won or made the frame in a Classic trial*

runs that season from the records of the last seven winners, they show 11 wins, a second and two thirds from 14 runs. That clearly points towards a high-performing filly who is just short of Group 1 standard.

Winners have been split equally between British and Irish stables over the past decade and in particular Aidan O'Brien has begun to exert his influence with two of the last four winners (he also had the runner-up in 2013).

Stables renowned for middle-distance Classic winners – and often backed by owner-breeders – have dominated.

The most recent upset was Mont Etoile at 25-1 in 2006 and none of the last 11 winners was outside the top five in the betting, with seven of them in the top two.

	FORM	WINNER	AGE & WGT	Adj RPR	SP	TRAINER	BEST RPR LAST 12 MONTHS (RUNS SINCE)
17	11-35	**Coronet**	3 9-0	114-9	9-1	John Gosden	3rd Prix Saint-Alary Gp1 (1m2f) (1)
16	31-3	**Even Song**	3 9-0	113-16	15-8f	Aidan O'Brien (IRE)	3rd Newmarket Listed (1m2f) (0)
15	8-111	**Curvy**	3 9-0	122-5	9-2	David Wachman (IRE)	won Curragh Gp3 (1m2f) (0)
14	81-10	**Bracelet**	3 9-0	119-7	10-1	Aidan O'Brien (IRE)	won Leopardstown Gp3 (7f) (1)
13	21	**Riposte** D	3 8-12	111-14	9-2	Lady Cecil	2nd Sandown Class 4 mdn (1m2f) (1)
12	8-11	**Princess Highway**	3 8-12	117-14	17-2	Dermot Weld (IRE)	won Naas Gp3 (1m2f) (0)
11	11151	**Banimpire** D	3 8-12	125T	3-1f	Jim Bolger (IRE)	5th Irish 1,000 Guineas Gp1 (1m) (1)
10	21-03	**Hibaayeb** C	3 8-12	125T	4-1j	Saeed Bin Suroor	won Fillies' Mile Gp1 (1m) (2)
09	11	**Flying Cloud**	3 8-12	120-3	5-1	Saeed Bin Suroor	won Saint-Cloud Gp3 (1m2½f) (0)
08	1-917	**Michita**	3 8-12	121T	10-3f	John Gosden	won Goodwood Listed (1m2f) (1)

Story of the last ten years

FAVOURITES: £3.71

TRAINERS IN THIS RACE (w-pl-r) Aidan O'Brien 2-1-13, John Gosden 2-5-21, Hugo Palmer 0-0-3, Ralph Beckett 0-1-7, Roger Varian 0-1-5, Sir Michael Stoute 0-3-9, William Haggas 0-0-5

FATE OF FAVOURITES: 1411244212 **POSITION OF WINNER IN MARKET:** 1311525214

EQUESTRIAN SURFACES LTD

GALLOP
WITH CONFIDENCE

TRAIN ON THE BEST

This is one of the crown jewels of Royal Ascot and the premier staying race of the British Flat season.

Despite the extreme distance of 2m4f, the race often produces an enthralling and thrilling contest – as it did last year when Big Orange and Order Of St George were separated by just a short-head after a ding-dong battle.

Another attractive element is that the best stayers often return year after year, and nine horses have won the race more than once in the 40-odd years since Sagaro, one of the greats, started his hat-trick in 1975.

That feat was eclipsed by the four-in-a-row of Yeats in 2006-2009, a sequence that marked the emergence of Aidan O'Brien as the dominant force of recent years. He has won seven of the last 12 runnings with four different horses and saddled the runner-up in three of the last five editions he didn't win.

This is a race where O'Brien habitually has a single representative and clearly his chosen one has to be taken seriously. His 12 runners since 2006 have returned form figures of 111121761212 and a level-stake profit of +8.7pt.

There is not a wide choice of targets for stayers and almost every recent winner has come down the Sagaro/

Story of the last ten years

FORM	WINNER	AGE & WGT	Adj RPR	SP	TRAINER	BEST RPR LAST 12 MONTHS (RUNS SINCE)
17 30-41	**Big Orange** C	6 9-2	131^{-3}	5-1	Michael Bell	won Princess of Wales's Gp2 (1m4f) (6)
16 111-1	**Order Of St George**	4 9-0	137^T	10-11f	Aidan O'Brien (IRE)	won Irish St Leger Gp1 (1m6f) (1)
15 41112	**Trip To Paris** C	4 9-0	121^{-10}	12-1	Ed Dunlop	2nd Henry II Stakes Gp3 (2m) (0)
14 110-1	**Leading Light** C	4 9-0	133^T	10-11f	Aidan O'Brien (IRE)	won Vintage Crop Stakes Gp3 (1m6f) (0)
13 133-1	**Estimate** C	4 8-11	126^{-4}	7-2f	Sir Michael Stoute	won Sagaro Stakes Gp3 (2m) (0)
12 133-1	**Colour Vision** C	4 9-0	134^T	6-1	Saeed Bin Suroor	won Sagaro Stakes Gp3 (2m) (0)
11 15-11	**Fame And Glory**	5 9-2	136^T	11-8f	Aidan O'Brien (IRE)	5th Prix de l'Arc de Triomphe Gp1 (1m4f) (2)
10 11-	**Rite Of Passage**	6 9-2	119^{-17}	20-1	Dermot Weld (IRE)	won Leopardstown hcap (2m) (0)
09 151-6	**Yeats** CD, BF	8 9-2	138^T	6-4f	Aidan O'Brien (IRE)	won Goodwood Cup Gp2 (2m) (3)
08 113-1	**Yeats** CD	7 9-2	136^T	11-8f	Aidan O'Brien (IRE)	won Irish St Leger Gp1 (1m6f) (2)

WINS-RUNS 4yo 5-8-43, 5yo 1-4-29, 6yo+ 4-8-53 **FAVOURITES** £7.18

TRAINERS IN THIS RACE Aidan O'Brien 5-3-10, Ed Dunlop 1-0-3, David Simcock 0-1-2, Hughie Morrison 0-0-4, Mick Channon 0-0-2

FATE OF FAVOURITES 1151011312 **POSITION OF WINNER IN MARKET** 1191411612

Big Orange's victory from Order Of St George (main picture) 12 months ago sparked huge celebrations

Henry II route in Britain or via the Vintage Crop/Saval Beg in Ireland. Eight of the last 11 winners had won at least one of those races en route and another had been runner-up in the Henry II.

The class factor is important, with 16 of the 18 winners since 2000 having previously struck in a Group 1 or Group 2 (11 had won at the highest level). Only the follow-up winners (Yeats and Royal Rebel) and 2005 winner Westerner had scored at this trip before, but just three (all trained by O'Brien) had yet to win over at least 2m.

Fancied runners have a good record. Only three of the 18 winners since 2000 were outside the top four in the market and 11 were in the top two.

Key trends

▸ *Sire stamina index in excess of 9.5f, 10/10*
▸ *Won within last two starts, 10/10*
▸ *Adjusted RPR of at least 126, 8/10*
▸ *Rated within 4lb of RPR top-rated, 8/10 (six were top-rated)*
▸ *Group-race winner, 8/10 (five had won a Group 1)*
  ▸ *Won over at least 2m, 8/10 (both exceptions trained by Aidan O'Brien)*

Other factors

▸ *Eight winners were competing in the race for the first time*
▸ *Winners of the Henry II Stakes finished 030023001; Yorkshire Cup 2067; Sagaro 0211727*
▸ *Six favourites have won in the last decade but Yeats was the only one to have previously won over the trip*

DID YOU KNOW?

Founded in 1807, the Gold Cup is the oldest race at Royal Ascot. Contrary to popular opinion it is not called the 'Ascot Gold Cup'

GOLD CUP

RECORD BREAKER

Yeats (2006, 2007, 2008 & 2009)
The only horse to win the Gold Cup four times; one-time Derby contender who also took the Coronation Cup at Epsom as a four-year-old; also won the Irish St Leger, Prix Royal-Oak and Goodwood Cup; became the oldest winner (aged eight) of the Gold Cup since Merman in 1900 when gaining his fourth success in 2009 and is commemorated with a statue in Ascot's parade ring

BETTING

Longest-priced winner: Indian Queen 25-1 (1991)

Shortest-priced winner: Ardross 1-5 (1981)

Market leaders: 27 favourites or joint favourites have been successful in 72 runnings

ROYAL FIRST

The Queen's Estimate made history in 2013 when becoming the first horse owned by a reigning monarch to win the Gold Cup. A half-sister to the 1999 Gold Cup winner Enzeli, Estimate also won the Queen's Vase at Royal Ascot in 2012

* All figures since 1946

WINNING CONNECTIONS

Most successful trainer
7 wins: Aidan O'Brien
Yeats (2006, 2007, 2008, 2009)
Fame And Glory (2011)
Leading Light (2014)
Order Of St George (2016)

Most successful jockey
11 wins: Lester Piggott
Zarathustra (1957)
Gladness (1958)
Pandofell (1961)
Twilight Alley (1963)
Fighting Charlie (1965)
Sagaro (1975, 1976, 1977)
Le Moss (1979)
Ardross (1981, 1982)

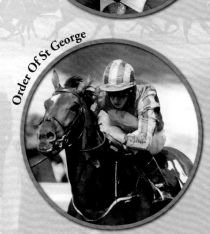

Order Of St George

Most successful owner
7 wins: Coolmore partners
Yeats (2006, 2007, 2008, 2009)
Fame And Glory (2011)
Leading Light (2014)
Order Of St George (2016)

This contest over the straight mile is the second of Royal Ascot's three heritage handicaps, sandwiched between the Royal Hunt Cup (Wednesday) and the Wokingham (Saturday), and is open to three-year-old colts and geldings.

Most winners have been lightly raced, with five of the last six having had no more than four outings, and the difficulty of weighing up a host of runners with limited form is reflected in the fact that four winners in the past decade were sent off at 20-1 or bigger and there has been only one winning favourite since 2006.

The only recent winner with a great deal of experience was War Envoy (12 runs) for Aidan O'Brien in 2015. He had run in four Group 1 races by then but most winners have been

restricted to maiden, novice and latterly handicap company, with every other winner in the past decade having run in a handicap before coming here. Six of them had won a handicap, four of them last time out.

A good level of form is important, with seven of the last ten winners no more than 3lb off the top on Racing Post Ratings (three of the last six were top) and another two only 6lb below.

Getting in on a weight just below 9st might be seen as ideal, with nine of the last 14 winners having been in the range from 8st 9lb to 8st 13lb.

An experienced, tactically astute jockey is a boon. Jamie Spencer has ridden the last two winners and four in total, while Ryan Moore also has two recent victories on Fast Or Free in 2012 and War Envoy *(pictured)* in 2015.

Key trends
▶ *Previously contested a handicap, 9/10 (six had won one)*
▶ *Officially rated 87-96, 9/10*
▶ *Carried no more than 9st 1lb, 9/10*
▶ *Rated within 6lb of RPR top-rated, 9/10 (three top)*
▶ *At least one top-three finish within last two starts, 8/10*
▶ *Won in current season over 7f or a mile, 8/10*

Other factors
▶ *John Gosden hasn't won this for a while but was successful four times between 1996 and 2001*

Story of the last ten years

	FORM	WINNER		AGE & WGT	OR		SP	TRAINER	BEST RPR LAST 12 MONTHS (RUNS SINCE)
17	2135	**Bless Him** D	3	8-9	90-6		25-1	David Simcock	5th Goodwood Class 2 hcap (7f) (0)
16	3-141	**Limitless** D	3	9-1	95T		13-2	Jamie Osborne	won Doncaster Class 4 hcap (1m) (0)
15	-2470	**War Envoy**	3	9-6	104T		10-1	Aidan O'Brien (IRE)	5th Prix Jean-Luc Lagardere Gp1 (7f) (5)
14	312	**Born In China** D	3	8-4	87-1		14-1	Andrew Balding	2nd Newmarket Class 2 hcap (1m) (0)
13	01-41	**Beauty Flame** D	3	8-12	96-6		20-1	Joanna Morgan (IRE)	won Curragh hcap (1m) (0)
12	6-11	**Fast Or Free** D	3	8-10	87T		6-1f	William Haggas	won Newmarket Class 3 hcap (1m) (0)
11	12-21	**Sagramor** D	3	8-13	93-2		8-1	Hughie Morrison	won Haydock Class 2 hcap (1m) (0)
10	71-12	**Ransom Note** D, BF	3	8-10	92-1		9-1	Barry Hills	2nd Newmarket Class 3 hcap (1m) (0)
09	2-315	**Fareer**	3	8-10	92-3		20-1	Ed Dunlop	won Chester Class 2 hcap (7½f) (1)
08	110-0	**Fifteen Love**	3	8-10	93-8		28-1	Roger Charlton	won Salisbury Class 4 (7f) (2)

FAVOURITES -£3.00

FATE OF FAVOURITES 0000144060 **POSITION OF WINNER IN MARKET** 0042186430

Like the preceding Britannia, this is a fascinating yet tricky handicap for three-year-olds but this one is over the longer trip of 1m4f and, unlike the Britannia, is open to fillies as well as colts and geldings.

Also in common with the Britannia, this race favours the bigger stables who have the strength in depth that gives them a better chance of housing the right type of lightly raced three-year-old.

Two of the trainers to watch in this and other 1m4f races are Mark Johnston (five winners since 1995) and Sir Michael Stoute (four since 1998). Another multiple winner is Roger Charlton, whose victory 12 months ago with Atty Persse came 25 years after his first with Source Of Light.

Godolphin trainers have won twice in the past four runnings (Saeed Bin Suroor with Elite Army in 2014 and

DID YOU KNOW?

More than 13,000 flowers and plants are grown and planted especially for Royal Ascot. Twelve groundstaff maintain the track, lawns and grounds year round and three more maintain the plants, shrubs, hedges and trees

Key trends
▶ *Carried no more than 9st 1lb, 9/10*
▶ *Top-three finish last time, 9/10*
▶ *Officially rated between 85 and 95, 9/10*
▶ *Previously contested a handicap, 9/10 (eight won one)*
▶ *Won earlier in the season, 8/10*
▶ *Drawn in double figures, 8/10*

Other factors
▶ *Only six winners had won over 1m2f-1m4f. Two of the other four were still maidens*
▶ *Since 1995, Mark Johnston has had five winners, while Sir Michael Stoute has had four*

Charlie Appleby with Space Age the following year).

John Gosden won twice in the 1990s but perhaps surprisingly he has failed to add to that tally – he went close with runner-up Space Ship in 2013 and it would not be a surprise if he had a strong challenger again.

The classy stayer Brown Panther in 2011 is the only recent winner who had raced this far before but one clue to potential stamina can be gleaned from two-year-old form. The last winner who had been unraced at two was Heron Bay in 2007 and eight of the ten winners since had been tried over 1m-1m2f as juveniles.

Eight of the winners in the past decade had been successful in handicaps, six of them last time out.

Since Cosmic Sun scored at 66-1 in 2009, six of the eight winners have come from the top four in the betting.

Story of the last ten years

FORM	WINNER	AGE	& WGT	OR	SP	TRAINER	BEST RPR LAST 12 MONTHS (RUNS SINCE)
17	1-12	**Atty Persse** BF	3	8-7	93-2	7-1	Roger Charlton	2nd Haydock Class 3 hcap (1m2f) (0)
16	21-11	**Gold Mount**	3	9-3	95-3	13-2	Alan King	won Sandown Class 3 hcap (1m2f) (0)
15	31-51	**Space Age**	3	8-10	88T	9-1	Charlie Appleby	won Newmarket Class 3 hcap (1m2f) (0)
14	1-31	**Elite Army**	3	9-1	94-5	4-1j	Saeed Bin Suroor	won Sandown Class 3 hcap (1m2f) (0)
13	4-322	**Elidor**	3	9-0	88-5	20-1	Mick Channon	2nd Lingfield Listed (1m3½f) (0)
12	12551	**Fennell Bay** (4ex)	3	8-1	85T	12-1	Mark Johnston	won Sandown Class 2 hcap (1m) (0)
11	1-411	**Brown Panther** D	3	8-13	91T	4-1j	Tom Dascombe	won Haydock Class 3 hcap (1m4f) (0)
10	2-111	**Dandino**	3	8-13	91-2	7-1	James Given	won Epsom Class 2 hcap (1m2f) (0)
09	24-09	**Cosmic Sun** (3oh)	3	7-12	80-6	66-1	Richard Fahey	2nd Ayr Class 2 hcap (1m) (3)
08	91-13	**Colony** BF	3	8-12	87T	11-2f	Sir Michael Stoute	3rd Newbury Class 2 hcap (1m2f) (0)

FAVOURITES £1.50 **FATE OF FAVOURITES:** 1451031000 **POSITION OF WINNER IN MARKET** 1031601432

THE QUEEN AND ROYAL ASCOT

Julian Muscat
on a special
relationship

At about this
time two years
ago, the
Queen's annual
appointment with Royal
Ascot will have been inked
into her diary for 2018. The
first entries are made 18
months in advance: they
include six days that are
ring-fenced each and every
year. Derby day is one,
together with all five days of
the royal meeting.

It has been thus since Her
Majesty, then Princess
Elizabeth, first attended the
meeting in 1945 at the age
of 19. She has hardly
missed a beat in the
intervening 73 years,
although affairs of state
have occasionally
complicated matters – in
1959, for example, the
Queen left mid-meeting
for a trip to Canada. The
odds against unearthing an
attendee of greater
longevity are extremely
remote. ▶

A lifetime of success

THE QUEEN'S 23 ROYAL ASCOT WINNERS

YEAR	RACE	HORSE	JOCKEY
1953	Royal Hunt Cup	CHOIR BOY	Doug Smith
1954	Hardwicke Stakes	AUREOLE	Eph Smith
	Rous Memorial Stakes	LANDAU	Sir Gordon Richards
1955	King George V Stakes	JARDINIERE	Doug Smith
1956	Royal Hunt Cup	ALEXANDER	Harry Carr
1957	Ribblesdale Stakes	ALMERIA	Harry Carr
	New Stakes	PALL MALL	Harry Carr
1958	Rous Memorial Stakes	SNOW CAT	Eph Smith
	King Edward VII Stakes	RESTORATION	Harry Carr
1959	St James's Palace Stakes	ABOVE SUSPICION	Harry Carr
	King Edward VII Stakes	PINDARI	Lester Piggott
1961	Coronation Stakes	AIMING HIGH	Lester Piggott
1968	Hardwicke Stakes	HOPEFUL VENTURE	Sandy Barclay
1970	Ascot Stakes	MAGNA CARTA	Geoff Lewis
1979	Queen's Vase	BUTTRESS	Willie Carson
	Ribblesdale Stakes	EXPANSIVE	Willie Carson
1992	Royal Hunt Cup	COLOUR SERGEANT	David Harrison
1995	Ribblesdale Stakes	PHANTOM GOLD	Frankie Dettori
1999	Duke of Edinburgh Stakes	BLUEPRINT	Gary Stevens
2008	Chesham Stakes	FREE AGENT	Richard Hughes
2012	Queen's Vase	ESTIMATE	Ryan Moore
2013	Gold Cup	ESTIMATE	Ryan Moore
2016	Hardwicke Stakes	DARTMOUTH	Olivier Peslier

The Queen at the royal meeting (clockwise from above): watching the action from the royal box in 2013; her famous colours hang in the weighing room; a pat for 2008 Chesham winner Free Agent; with the Gold Cup trophy after winning the race with Estimate in 2013; in the parade ring in 2014 with (from left) her racing adviser John Warren, Princess Anne, Ryan Moore and Sir Michael Stoute

She has celebrated doubles aplenty among 23 winners in all. There has been angst and elation, and raised eyebrows in 1952 when the royal hope, Choir Boy, started favourite for the Royal Hunt Cup. Choir Boy finished plumb last, prompting the princess to erupt in uncontrollable laughter.

She puts the 'royal' into Royal Ascot, of course, but not just by birthright. For many, Her Majesty's presence at the races is the daily highlight. Larger crowds are drawn to the winner's enclosure for the conclusion to the royal procession than for any winner over the five days.

Ascot is also where the Queen is at her most relaxed. She is invariably smiling, rejoicing in an annual rite that defines the British summer. It is here that she brings to life the words of the late Sir Peter O'Sullevan, who vividly described her as "a very human being".

Royal winners at Royal Ascot have been increasingly hard to come by. There was a flurry of them in the years immediately after the coronation. In that year, 1953, Choir Boy atoned handsomely for his flop the previous year by landing the Hunt Cup.

Her Majesty visited the winner's enclosure in each of the next six years. By the end of the decade she had made that walk 11 times. They were the best of times; by contrast, there were five winners over the next two decades, and seven more from 1980 to the present day.

Foremost among them was Estimate's emotional triumph in the 2013 Gold Cup. There was rejoicing in the royal box as Ryan Moore drove the super-game filly to a narrow verdict, after which the Queen said the Gold Cup was the race above all others that she had yearned to win. Estimate remains the only horse to win twice at Royal Ascot for Her Majesty, having also landed the 2012 Queen's Vase.

The Hunt Cup, Ribblesdale and Hardwicke

Stakes have been kindest to the Queen. She has won each of them three times. Dartmouth's Hardwicke triumph in 2016, which hoisted the hat-trick, was her most recent winner at the meeting.

The British monarchy is celebrated annually in the race names at Royal Ascot. Queen Anne established racing at the venue more than 300 years ago; her legacy is commemorated by the Queen Anne Stakes, which traditionally opens the five-day meeting. Queen Mary, Queen Alexandra, George V and Edward VII are other ancestors of the Queen to have races named after them at Royal Ascot, while Queen Victoria donated the trophy on the Queen's Vase's inauguration in 1838.

As for Her Majesty, she lends her name to the Queen Elizabeth II Stakes, at Ascot on Champions Day. It is inconceivable she will not be commemorated at the appropriate time by a race at a meeting she has graced for longer than she has reigned.

THE QUEEN AND ROYAL ASCOT

ONE of the most magnificent sights of a day at Royal Ascot is the royal procession, which brings the Queen and her guests along the straight mile in four horse-drawn carriages, parading in front of the vast crowds before turning under the grandstand and into the parade ring.

The royal party leave Windsor Castle after lunch and are driven by car to Windsor Great Park, where they transfer to the carriages. They start the procession along the course at 2pm precisely, with racing commencing at 2.30, and a different path is chosen each day, to protect the ground. As the procession reaches the grandstand, the national

The royal procession

anthem is played by a guards band. Each landau carriage carries four people, with the Queen at the head of the group. The carriages are pulled by Windsor greys and bays, mainly Cleveland bays, who are trained as carriage horses from the age of four and work for approximately 15 years.

Ascot racecourse traces its origins back to 1711 when Queen Anne rode out from Windsor Castle and declared this area of East Cote "ideal for horses to gallop at full stretch". The first royal meeting took place at Ascot in 1768, although the royal procession did not start until 1825 during the reign of King George IV. Initially it took place on only one day of the meeting before it was first extended to all days in 1919, in celebration of victory in the First World War.

There have been a few interruptions along the way. In 1929 King George V was absent with illness, in 1964 and again in 1971 there were cancellations due to bad weather, and political events stopped the spectacle

in 1970 when there was a general election on the Thursday and in 2001 for the state opening of parliament. For the most part, however, the pageantry of the royal procession has been an integral part of the day's entertainment and undoubtedly this grandest of entrances is part of what makes Royal Ascot so special.

DAY FOUR

When it comes to Royal Ascot, that Friday feeling is a great one to have.

Aside from the opening afternoon, Ascot's fourth day is the only one to feature multiple Group 1 prizes. The Friday can also claim to have the meeting's newest top-flight contest, a race that has hit the ground running almost as fast as the horses who take part.

The Commonwealth Cup was launched in 2015 as part of the sport's attempt to reinvigorate racing's sprinting division and it has been a roaring success.

The inaugural winner Muhaarar looked special on the day and even more special thereafter, mopping up three further Group 1 prizes, including back at Ascot on British Champions Day.

Quiet Reflection was another excellent winner in 2016, while in 2017 the race was arguably the most eagerly anticipated of the week and lived up to its billing, with Caravaggio defeating subsequent champion sprinter Harry Angel in an epic showdown.

The same Coolmore connections who struck with Caravaggio were last year also successful in Friday's second Group 1, the Coronation Stakes, with Winter.

This is the fillies' equivalent of the St James's Palace Stakes and often the place where winners of the major Guineas in Britain, France and Ireland collide. It is an historic event that brings together various strands of form and goes a long way to determining the best of the best.

Fillies get plenty of opportunities on Ascot Friday, with the post-procession fare kicking off with the Albany Stakes, an important prize for two-year-olds. If that can be difficult to solve, even harder is the Sandringham Handicap, a cavalry charge for three-year-old fillies up the straight mile that in 2017 went to American raider Con Te Partiro.

The afternoon's other two races are both staged over the blue riband distance of a mile and a half, yet they cater for very different horses.

The King Edward VII Stakes, commonly referred to as the Ascot Derby, gives colts who failed to win the most famous of the Flat's crown jewels the chance of valuable compensation. That has proved to be the case in the last two runnings, won by Across The Stars and Permian, both of whom went to Ascot after finishing tenth at Epsom.

The clue to the card-closing Duke of Edinburgh Handicap is Sir Michael Stoute, successful in six of the last 20 editions. Expect him to have something towards the top of the betting again. Stoute loves that Friday feeling.

Friday June 22

RUNNING ORDER

2.30 Albany Stakes (Group 3) *Last year's winner: Different League 20-1*	**6f** 2yo fillies	£90,000
3.05 King Edward VII Stakes (Group 2) *Last year's winner: Permian 6-1*	**1m4f** 3yo colts and geldings	£225,000
3.40 Commonwealth Cup (Group 1) *Last year's winner: Caravaggio 5-6f*	**6f** 3yo	£500,000
4.20 Coronation Stakes (Group 1) *Last year's winner: Winter 4-9f*	**1m** 3yo fillies	£500,000
5.00 Sandringham Stakes (Handicap) *Last year's winner: Con Te Partiro 20-1*	**1m** 3yo fillies	£90,000
5.35 Duke of Edinburgh Stakes (Handicap) *Last year's winner: Rare Rhythm 20-1*	**1m4f** 3yo+	£90,000

Race value is total prize-money

This Group 3 for two-year-old fillies was established in 2002 at Listed level and initially run as the Henry Carnarvon Stakes in memory of the Queen's racing manager, who died the previous year.

Upgraded in 2015, the 6f contest is invariably won by a precocious juvenile who lacks the scope to train on and scale the heights at three. Although several winners have gone on to better things in their two-year-old days – Cursory Glance won the Group 1 Moyglare Stud Stakes and Brave Anna took the Group 1 Cheveley Park Stakes – for many the Albany is their career highlight.

All of the last ten winners

Key trends
▶ *One or two runs, 10/10*
▶ *Adjusted RPR of at least 95, 10/10*
▶ *Shed maiden tag, 9/10*
▶ *By a sire with a stamina index of at least 7.4f, 9/10*
▶ *Ran in a maiden last time out, 7/10*

Other factors
▶ *Two winners were top-rated but the other eight were between 9lb and 22lb off the top*
▶ *The two maidens to have won since 2007 were both trained by Mick Channon*

Jamie Spencer celebrates his 2013 win on Kiyoshi

had raced at least once and an RPR of at least 95 has been essential in that period.

It has not been a great race for favourites, however. Since Cuis Ghaire triumphed at 8-11 in 2008, only two market leaders have been successful – Newfangled (7-4) and Illuminate (4-1).

Five of the last ten winners have been returned at odds of 14-1 or bigger and that trend has become more pronounced lately, with three of the last four scorers sent off at 14-1, 16-1 and 20-1.

Jamie Spencer is the jockey with the best record in the race with four wins – La Chunga (2005), Nijoom Dubai (2007), Samitar (2011) and Kiyoshi (2013) – while Mick Channon, who trained Nijoom Dubai and Samitar, also struck with Silca's Gift (2003), making him the leading trainer.

Story of the last ten years

	FORM	WINNER	AGE & WGT	Adj RPR	SP	TRAINER	BEST RPR LAST 12 MONTHS (RUNS SINCE)
17	11	**Different League** D	2 9-0	96-18	20-1	Matthieu Palussiere (FR)	won Angers conditions stakes (6f) (0)
16	81	**Brave Anna** D	2 9-0	103-14	16-1	Aidan O'Brien (IRE)	won Curragh mdn (6f) (0)
15	1	**Illuminate**	2 9-0	98-12	4-1f	Richard Hannon	won Salisbury Class 3 (5f) (0)
14	1	**Cursory Glance** D	2 9-0	98-10	14-1	Roger Varian	won Kempton Class 5 mdn (6f) (0)
13	41	**Kiyoshi** D	2 8-12	106-15	8-1	Charlie Hills	won Goodwood Class 5 mdn (6f) (0)
12	1	**Newfangled** D	2 8-12	111T	7-4f	John Gosden	won Newmarket Class 4 mdn (6f) (0)
11	3	**Samitar**	2 8-12	95-22	16-1	Mick Channon	3rd Newmarket Class 4 mdn (6f) (0)
10	1	**Memory** D	2 8-12	107-9	15-2	Richard Hannon snr	won Goodwood Class 5 mdn (6f) (0)
09	31	**Habaayib** D	2 8-12	102-16	16-1	Ed Dunlop	won Nottingham Class 5 mdn auct (5f) (0)
08	11	**Cuis Ghaire** D	2 8-12	121T	8-11f	Jim Bolger (IRE)	won Naas Gp3 (6f) (0)

FAVOURITES -£0.52

TRAINERS IN THIS RACE (w-pl-r) Aidan O'Brien 1-1-9, Ed Dunlop 1-0-3, Richard Hannon 1-0-5, Roger Varian 1-0-3, David Evans 0-1-1, James Given 0-0-2, Jeremy Noseda 0-2-5, Keith Dalgleish 0-0-2, Mark Johnston 0-0-7, Wesley Ward 0-1-7, William Haggas 0-0-3

FATE OF FAVOURITES 1240123152 **POSITION OF WINNER IN MARKET** 1548137179

RoR
Retraining of Racehorses

Racing to a new career at ror.org.uk

RoR
Retraining of Racehorses

Source a Horse

sourceahorse.ror.org.uk

A new website for selling or loaning a horse directly out of a trainer's yard and for all former racehorses.

Owner/Trainer Helpline

A dedicated helpline to assist in the placement of horses coming out of training.

Rehoming Direct

RoR has compiled a checklist to safeguard your horse's future when moved directly into the sport horse market.

Visit
ror.org.uk
for rehoming options and advice

Retrainers

RoR has a list of retrainers recommended by trainers who can start the retraining process and assess each horse.

Equine Charities

Retrain former racehorses for a donation, as well as care for vulnerable horses with the help of RoR funding.

RoR is British horseracing's official charity for the welfare of horses retired from racing.

T: 01488 648998

This Group 2 over 1m4f for three-year-olds comes just under three weeks after the Derby at Epsom and was once officially called the Ascot Derby, as it still is colloquially, such is the close link between the races.

Even though there is only a short time between Epsom and Royal Ascot, many King Edward VII winners have graduated from the Derby, including the last two, Across The Stars and Permian, who both finished tenth there.

Favourites have a poor recent record – only Nathaniel at 11-4 in 2011 has justified market leadership in the last 11 runnings – and winners can come from recognised Classic trials or handicaps (Hillstar in 2013 and Eagle Top in 2014 were both

DID YOU KNOW?
There are more than 100 bars and food outlets around the racecourse and 225 private boxes, with 39 professional kitchens operating during Royal Ascot

Key trends
▸ *Adjusted RPR of at least 120, 8/10*
▸ *Yet to win at 1m4f, 8/10*
▸ *Within 10lb of RPR top-rated, 8/10*
▸ *Ran in a recognised Derby trial, 7/10 (two won)*
▸ *Won earlier in the season over 1m1f-1m3f, 6/10*

Other factors
▸ *No winner had run in Group company at two*
▸ *Three winners achieved a top-three finish in the Lingfield Derby Trial, one was placed in the Chester Vase and one won the Dante*

having their first start in Group company).

Sir Michael Stoute, who had his first success in 1983 with Shareef Dancer, must always be respected, having won seven times. Along with two winners, he has had a second, third and fourth in the eight runnings since 2010.

Mark Johnston and John Gosden have had three winners apiece. Gosden's best winner was Nathaniel, who went on to great success at Group 1 level. Since then, Gosden has had seven runners with one win, two seconds and a third.

Frankie Dettori has had four winners – most recently on the Stoute-trained Across The Stars in 2016 – and William Buick has won three times since 2011 (twice for Gosden and once for Johnston).

Story of the last ten years

	FORM	WINNER	AGE & WGT	Adj RPR	SP	TRAINER	BEST RPR LAST 12 MONTHS (RUNS SINCE)
17	32110	**Permian**	3 9-0	128^T	6-1	Mark Johnston	won Dante Stakes Gp2 (1m2½f) (1)
16	2-130	**Across The Stars** D	3 9-0	120^{-2}	7-1	Sir Michael Stoute	3rd Lingfield Derby Trial Listed (1m3½f) (1)
15	1-2	**Balios**	3 9-0	123^{-5}	3-1	David Simcock	2nd Newmarket Stakes Listed (1m2f) (0)
14	14	**Eagle Top** BF	3 9-0	114^{-10}	12-1	John Gosden	4th Leicester Class 3 hcap (1m4f) (0)
13	41-22	**Hillstar** BF	3 8-12	118^{-13}	15-2	Sir Michael Stoute	2nd Newbury Class 2 hcap (1m2f) (0)
12	01-51	**Thomas Chippendale**	3 8-12	122^{-13}	9-2	Sir Henry Cecil	won Newmarket Class 3 hcap (1m2f) (0)
11	22-12	**Nathaniel** D, BF	3 8-12	127^T	11-4f	John Gosden	2nd Chester Vase Gp3 (1m4½f) (0)
10	11121	**Monterosso**	3 8-12	126^{-7}	7-2	Mark Johnston	won Newmarket Class 2 hcap (1m2f) (0)
09	1-332	**Father Time** BF	3 8-12	123^{-5}	9-1	Sir Henry Cecil	2nd Fairway Stakes Listed (1m2f) (0)
08	0-113	**Campanologist** BF	3 8-12	125^{-6}	9-1	Saeed Bin Suroor	won Feilden Stakes Listed (1m1f) (1)

FAVOURITES -£6.25

TRAINERS IN THIS RACE (w-pl-r) John Gosden 2-4-12, Mark Johnston 2-0-4, Sir Michael Stoute 2-3-7, Saeed Bin Suroor 1-0-3, Aidan O'Brien 0-5-13, Brian Meehan 0-0-2, Charlie Appleby 0-0-2, Ralph Beckett 0-0-3, William Haggas 0-0-3

FATE OF FAVOURITES 2641422P23 **POSITION OF WINNER IN MARKET** 6621336242

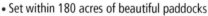

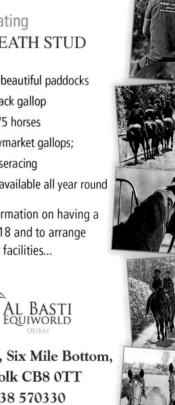
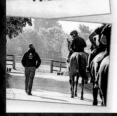

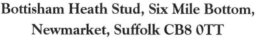

This sprint for three-year-olds was introduced in 2015, with the aim of allowing them to compete at the top level against their contemporaries without having to take on older horses at such an early stage of the season. At the same time the Diamond Jubilee Stakes, another Group 1 Royal Ascot sprint, was closed to three-year-olds.

The new race has proved a huge success, attracting top-class fields in its three runnings and offering a high-level stepping stone to races such as the July Cup and Nunthorpe Stakes where the older horses lie in wait.

Obviously it is hard to find discernible trends with such a lack of data, but two things already stand out.

Favourites have done well, with two of the three winners – Quiet Reflection and Caravaggio – sent off market leader. And the second point is that plenty of proven first-place form in Group company – in one or more two-year-old races over 5f and 6f, or in that year's

The story so far

	FORM	WINNER	AGE & WGT	Adj RPR	SP	TRAINER	BEST RPR LAST 12 MONTHS (RUNS SINCE)
17	111-1	**Caravaggio** CD	3 9-3	131ᵀ	5-6f	Aidan O'Brien (IRE)	won Naas Gp3 (6f) (0)
16	11-11	**Quiet Reflection** D	3 9-0	130ᵀ	7-4f	Karl Burke	won Haydock Gp2 (6f) (0)
15	13-18	**Muhaarar** D	3 9-3	128⁻³	10-1	Charlie Hills	won Greenham Stakes Gp3 (7f) (1)

FAVOURITES £1.58

TRAINERS IN THIS RACE (w-pl-r) Aidan O'Brien 1-1-4, Karl Burke 1-0-1, Charlie Hills 1-0-2, Clive Cox 0-1-3, Henry Candy 0-1-2, Charlie Appleby 0-1-2, Wesley Ward 0-0-2, Richard Hannon 0-0-5

FATE OF FAVOURITES 011 **POSITION OF WINNER IN MARKET** 611

Cup winners (clockwise from main): Caravaggio, Muhaarar (left), Quiet Reflection and 2016's successful trainer Karl Burke

early sprints – is a strong indicator.

Inaugural winner Muhaarar had landed the Group 2 Gimcrack Stakes at York during his two-year-old career before taking the Group 3 Greenham Stakes on his reappearance at three (recording a then career-best RPR of 119).

Quiet Reflection, the 2016 winner, had taken the Group 3 Cornwallis Stakes at Ascot as a juvenile and won the Group 2 Sandy Lane Stakes at Haydock (RPR 116) three weeks before Royal Ascot, while Caravaggio went into his hugely trumpeted clash with Harry Angel and Blue Point 12 months ago unbeaten in five starts.

Four of those came in Caravaggio's juvenile career, including Royal Ascot's Group 2 Coventry Stakes and the Group 1 Phoenix Stakes at the Curragh, and he started last season with a Group 3 success at Naas (RPR 121).

As a result of their achievements before Royal Ascot, Quiet Reflection and Caravaggio were both

DID YOU KNOW?

Jockeys at Ascot are called to mount by a bell in the parade ring and, unique to Ascot, a bell is also rung as the horses swing into the straight for races run on the round course

top-rated on RPR, while Muhaarar was only 3lb off the top.

This race is notable as the only Group 1 in Britain for three-year-olds that allows geldings to compete, although no gelding has been successful in the first three runnings.

DAY FOUR

This is the premier race for three-year-old fillies at Royal Ascot and has held Group 1 status since 1988. Like its counterpart for colts, the St James's Palace Stakes, this race often provides a clash between Guineas participants from Britain, Ireland and France and has been won by some of the best female milers during its long and illustrious history.

Last year Winter won the 1,000 Guineas at Newmarket and the Irish 1,000 Guineas at the Curragh before justifying odds of 4-9 here with a two-and-a-quarter-length success over Roly Poly. She was the first to complete that prestigious treble since Mark Johnston's Attraction in 2004.

All but one of the 18 winners since 2000 had run in a Guineas, with seven having been successful in at least one of those Classics and four more placed (the one who hadn't competed in a Guineas was Fallen For You in 2012).

Many winners also achieved a high level of form as juveniles. With any runner who hasn't won a Guineas, the next best indicator is a Group 1 placing at two – 15 of the last 18 winners fell into one of those two categories. Ten of the 18 were either a Guineas winner or a Group 1 winner at two, though only 2013 winner Sky Lantern was both.

Story of the last ten years

	FORM	WINNER	AGE & WGT	Adj RPR	SP	TRAINER	BEST RPR LAST 12 MONTHS (RUNS SINCE)
17	1-211	**Winter** D	3 9-0	133ᵀ	4-9f	Aidan O'Brien (IRE)	won Irish 1,000 Guineas Gp1 (1m) (0)
16	13-13	**Qemah** D, BF	3 9-0	127⁻⁴	6-1	Jean-Claude Rouget (FR)	won Chantilly Gp3 (1m) (1)
15	32-11	**Ervedya** D	3 9-0	129⁻¹	3-1	Jean-Claude Rouget (FR)	won Maisons-Laffitte Gp3 (7f) (1)
14	312-7	**Rizeena** C	3 9-0	127ᵀ	11-2	Clive Brittain	won Moyglare Stud Stakes Gp1 (7f) (2)
13	18-21	**Sky Lantern** D	3 9-0	127ᵀ	9-2j	Richard Hannon snr	won 1,000 Guineas Gp1 (1m) (0)
12	25-16	**Fallen For You** D, BF	3 9-0	125⁻⁷	12-1	John Gosden	2nd May Hill Stakes Gp2 (1m) (3)
11	2-401	**Immortal Verse** D	3 9-0	123⁻⁵	8-1	Robert Collet (FR)	won Chantilly Gp2 (1m) (0)
10	318-5	**Lillie Langtry** D	3 9-0	123⁻⁴	7-2f	Aidan O'Brien (IRE)	5th Irish 1,000 Guineas Gp1 (1m) (0)
09	31-1	**Ghanaati** D	3 9-0	131ᵀ	2-1f	Barry Hills	won 1,000 Guineas Gp1 (1m) (0)
08	-7615	**Lush Lashes** BF	3 9-0	127⁻²	5-1	Jim Bolger (IRE)	won Musidora Stakes Gp2 (1m½f) (1)

FAVOURITES £1.69

TRAINERS IN THIS RACE (w-pl-r) Aidan O'Brien 2-3-13, John Gosden 1-3-9

FATE OF FAVOURITES 4115010261 **POSITION OF WINNER IN MARKET** 2114613241

Sir Michael Stoute, who landed his first Coronation with the brilliant Sonic Lady in 1986, has won four times, while Winter's trainer Aidan O'Brien has been successful on three occasions.

Ryan Moore is the most successful jockey in the race's recent history. He has steered home two of the last four winners, Rizeena (2014) and Winter.

There has been a growing trend in recent years for winners of the race to be trained outside Britain. Six of the last ten fall into that category, with three Irish winners and three French-based scorers, two of whom were prepared by Jean-Claude Rouget.

Both of Rouget's fillies had contested the Group 1 Poule

d'Essai des Pouliches (the French 1,000 Guineas) on their previous start – Ervedya won and Qemah finished third.

This is not the only time in the race's history when overseas raiders have been to the fore. During the period 1989-1996 the race was won by French stables on three occasions (Andre Fabre, Criquette Head and Elie Lellouche) and by two Irish yards (Michael Kauntze and John Oxx).

Fallen For You, who bucks the trends in more ways than one, is the only winner since 2000 who wasn't in the first four in the betting and the only one sent off bigger than 8-1. Half of the 18 winners in that period were favourite or joint-favourite.

Qemah storms home to win the 2016 Coronation Stakes

Key trends
▶ *Adjusted Racing Post Rating of at least 123, 10/10*
▶ *Rated within 7lb of RPR top-rated, 10/10*
▶ *Ran in a European 1,000 Guineas, 9/10*
▶ *Won earlier in the season, 8/10*

Other factors
▶ *Five winners had run in the 1,000 Guineas, where they finished 61171; three ran in France (013) and two in Ireland (51)*
▶ *Winners of the Irish 1,000 Guineas finished 73834161*
▶ *Only four winners had won a Group race as a juvenile*

CORONATION STAKES

STAR WINNERS

Pretty Polly (1904)
One of the greatest fillies of all time and winner of 22 of her 24 races, including the 1,000 Guineas, Oaks and St Leger

Meld (1955)
Winner of the fillies' Triple Crown with victories in the 1,000 Guineas, Oaks and St Leger; dam of 1966 Derby winner Charlottown

Attraction (2004)
One of the few fillies to win the 1,000 Guineas, Irish 1,000 Guineas and Coronation Stakes; also won the Queen Mary Stakes at Royal Ascot

BETTING

Longest-priced winner: Rebecca Sharp 25-1 (1997)

Shortest-priced winner: Humble Duty 1-33 (1970)

Market leaders: 31 favourites or joint favourites have been successful in 72 runnings

CLASSIC HEROINES

The last five 1,000 Guineas winners who went on to land the Coronation

Russian Rhythm (2003)
Attraction (2004)
Ghanaati (2009)
Sky Lantern (2013)
Winter (2017)

All figures since 1946

WINNING CONNECTIONS

Most successful trainer
5 wins: Sir Henry Cecil
Roussalka (1975)
One In A Million (1979)
Chalon (1982)
Chimes Of Freedom (1990)
Kissing Cousin (1994)

Lester Piggott

Most successful jockeys
4 wins: Joe Mercer
Festoon (1954), Rosalba (1959)
Haymaking (1966)
One In A Million (1979)

4 wins: Lester Piggott
Aiming High (1961), Lisadell (1974)
Roussalka (1975), Chalon (1982)

4 wins: Walter Swinburn
Sonic Lady (1986), Milligram (1987)
Marling (1992), Exclusive (1998)

Sheikh Mohammed

Most successful owners
3 wins: Sheikh Mohammed
Sonic Lady (1986)
Golden Opinion (1989)
Kissing Cousin (1994)

3 wins: Cheveley Park Stud
Exclusive (1998)
Russian Rhythm (2003)
Nannina (2006)

3 wins: Coolmore partners
Sophisticat (2002), Lillie Langtry (2010), Winter (2017)

The Sandringham, which was introduced to the Royal Ascot programme in 2005 and is now effectively a fillies' Britannia, moves from Wednesday to Friday this year. This brings it into line with the feature handicaps on each day being run as race five, arguably the most betting-friendly position for such races.

The race is restricted to three-year-old fillies and is almost always won by a progressive type. Nine of the 13 winners since 2005 had already tasted success that season (six were last-time-out winners) and Muteela (2014) and Persuasive (2016) both went to Royal Ascot unbeaten in three previous starts, which included success on the all-weather.

A mark of the developing talent that often comes to the fore here is that

Key trends
▶ *Lost maiden tag, 10/10*
▶ *Carried no more than 9st 2lb, 7/10*
▶ *Officially rated 94-104, 7/10*
▶ *Won over 7f or 1m earlier that season, 6/10*
▶ *Contested Group/Listed race as a three-year-old, 6/10*

Other factors
▶ *Four winners ran in handicaps as three-year-olds (all four won at least one)*
▶ *No winner has been more than 1lb out of the handicap*
▶ *Two winners had been unplaced in Classics*

Persuasive, who won the Sandringham off an official mark of 95, signed off her career the following year by landing the Group 1 Queen Elizabeth II Stakes. Another subsequent Group 1 scorer was 2006 winner Red Evie, who went on to land the Matron and Lockinge Stakes.

Despite the large number of runners and hugely competitive nature of the Sandringham, it is notable that fancied contenders do well. Eight of the last 13 winners came from the top two in the betting, including five who had at least a share of favouritism.

Before last year's 20-1 US-trained winner Con Te Partiro, only one other scorer since 2005 had been bigger than 11-1.

It is also worth noting that eight of the last 13 winners had already won over a mile or further, which is clearly good preparation for this fast-paced and testing race.

Frankie Dettori's mount is always worth a second glance – he has won the race seven times, though only twice since it became part of Royal Ascot. Jamie Spencer has ridden the winner on three occasions, all at the royal meeting.

Story of the last ten years

	FORM	WINNER	AGE & WGT	OR	SP	TRAINER	BEST RPR LAST 12 MONTHS (RUNS SINCE)
17	142-4	Con Te Partiro	3 9-5	102-12	20-1	Wesley Ward (USA)	4th Belmont Park Listed (7f) (0)
16	1-11	Persuasive	3 8-9	95^T	11-4f	John Gosden	won Chelmsford Class 2 hcp (1m) (0)
15	13-17	Osaila CD	3 9-7	107-3	13-2	Richard Hannon	5th Moyglare Stud Stakes Gp1 (7f) (4)
14	1-11	Muteela	3 8-13	95^T	9-2f	Mark Johnston	won Newmarket Class 3 hcap (1m) (0)
13	41-61	Annecdote (1oh)	3 8-7	91^T	11-1	Jonathan Portman	won Newbury Class 4 hcap (7f) (0)
12	6-14	Duntle	3 9-2	104^T	4-1f	David Wachman (IRE)	4th Leopardstown Gp3 (1m) (0)
11	0-512	Rhythm Of Light	3 8-12	94^T	8-1	Tom Dascombe	2nd Haydock Class 3 hcap (7f) (0)
10	1-428	Timepiece CD	3 9-5	105-4	5-1	Sir Henry Cecil	2nd Lingfield Listed (1m3½f) (1)
09	4-531	Moneycantbuymelove	3 8-11	96^T	9-2f	Michael Bell	won Goodwood Listed (1m2f) (0)
08	15-33	Festivale	3 9-1	94-6	10-1	John Dunlop	3rd York Listed (1m) (0)

FAVOURITES £9.75

FATE OF FAVOURITES 0132101210 **POSITION OF WINNER IN MARKET** 6125151219

5.35 Duke of Edinburgh Stakes

This prestigious and valuable 1m4f handicap for three-year-olds and upwards dates back to 1914 and was known as the Bessborough Handicap before being renamed in 1999.

Winners of this race sometimes go on to make a splash in Listed and Group company, with Blueprint (1999) taking the Group 2 Jockey Club Stakes the following year and Young Mick (2006) landing the Group 3 Cumberland Lodge Stakes.

Four-year-olds have the best record, with 14 of the last 20 winners, although the last two runnings have gone to five-year-olds.

Sir Michael Stoute has a long and successful history with the race, having had six winners, while Mark Johnston and Hughie Morrison are two other trainers to note. Remarkably, those three have had 12 of the last 20 winners between them.

The 1m4f handicaps at Newmarket's Guineas meeting and York's Dante fixture often provide good guides. Since the last Irish-trained winner (Katiykha in 2000), 11 of the 17 winners had form at one of those meetings and nine of those had achieved a top-six placing (though only two won).

A good run at Epsom's Derby meeting or the Goodwood trials fixture in mid-May is also worth noting, while three of the last nine winners had been deemed good enough to run at Royal Ascot the previous year (finishing no better than fifth).

Trouble in running in maximum fields on Ascot's round course is a common occurrence and it is no real surprise that the winner has been returned at 10-1 or bigger in 16 of the last 30 runnings, with Rare Rhythm (pictured) (20-1 last year) being the latest.

Key trends
► Aged four or five, 10/10
► Officially rated between 91 and 101, 9/10
► Achieved best RPR in a Class 2 or 3 handicap, 9/10
► Drawn in double figures, 9/10
► Top-three finish last time, 9/10 (four won)
► Ran no more than four times that season, 8/10 (both exceptions trained by Mark Johnston)

Other factors
► Three of the last five winners started favourite, including one joint favourite

Story of the last ten years

	FORM	WINNER		AGE & WGT	OR	SP	TRAINER	BEST RPR LAST 12 MONTHS (RUNS SINCE)
17	171/8-	Rare Rhythm D		5 9-2	97-4	20-1	Charlie Appleby	Seasonal debut (0)
16	22-01	Kinema		5 9-4	99-3	8-1	Ralph Beckett	won Goodwood Class 2 hcap (1m6f) (0)
15	342-3	Arab Dawn BF		4 9-2	96T	6-1j	Hughie Morrison	3rd Newmarket Class 2 hcap (1m4f) (0)
14	2-111	Arab Spring D		4 9-10	104-3	11-4f	Sir Michael Stoute	won York Class 2 hcap (1m4f) (0)
13	010-3	Opinion		4 9-0	95T	8-1	Sir Michael Stoute	3rd Newmarket Class 2 hcap (1m4f) (0)
12	-1061	Camborne D		4 9-4	97-1	11-2f	John Gosden	won Doncaster Class 4 hcap (1m4f) (0)
11	21641	Fox Hunt D		4 9-8	99-2	12-1	Mark Johnston	2nd Chester Class 2 hcap (1m2½f) (6)
10	67-42	Cill Rialaig C		5 8-11	91-3	16-1	Hughie Morrison	2nd Epsom Class 2 hcap (1m4f) (0)
09	83332	Drill Sergeant		4 9-7	101-3	14-1	Mark Johnston	3rd Jockey Club Stakes Gp2 (1m4f) (3)
08	23-13	Sugar Ray D, BF		4 9-0	95-8	8-1	Sir Michael Stoute	3rd York Class 2 hcap (1m4f) (0)

WINS-PL-RUNS 4yo 7-15-92, 5yo 3-10-50, 6yo+ 0-4-34 **FAVOURITES** £3.75

FATE OF FAVOURITES 2020121120 **POSITION OF WINNER IN MARKET** 3878151148

Ascot Racecourse with some astute predictions

oyal Ascot is the perfect excuse to dress in your finest and enjoy the summer's biggest social event.

Fashion is integral to the week and the Royal Ascot Style Guide plays a pivotal role in predicting key trends for the summer season, providing inspiration to racegoers keen to dress in style while keeping in line with the famous dress code.

This season's introduction of dress codes and style suggestions for the Village and Windsor Enclosures provides our guests with fashionable looks for each of the four enclosures, ensuring every racegoer can enjoy the occasion in style.

The varying dress codes across the enclosures means different requirements and recommendations for each area. We predict this season's midi trend will inspire women to pick elegant dresses and skirts, particularly in the Royal Enclosure. For trackside areas such as the Village, the terrain calls for shoes with a wedge heel and a sturdy hat or fascinator, so we look forward to seeing how our guests interpret this style.

For ladies, we envisage an array of this season's biggest trend: the polka dot. This print suits a myriad of dresses, skirts and jumpsuits as shown in this year's Style Guide.

For gentlemen, we predict suave and sophisticated suits that play with colour and print in the Queen Anne, Village and Windsor Enclosures. But nothing quite beats the sophistication of the classic morning suits worn by gentlemen in the Royal Enclosure.

Award-winning milliner Katherine Elizabeth says go bold

I love to dress up and this year is all about being a little bit wild, so why not be bold and buy yourself a colourful dress and a fancy hat to match?

This year we are seeing uplifting, joyous fashion featuring rainbow colours – tomato red is very in and so is a splash of orange. Cobalt, emerald green and bright yellow are also still big.

Don't be afraid to wear bold, bright colours. They look great in the sun and will enhance the colour of your eyes, skin and hair for maximum impact.

I have created lots of bright-coloured hats this season, mixing cobalt blue with canary yellow and red with orange or a splash of emerald green and red.

Hats that are trendy have a hint of nature with leaves, flowers and organic material. Remember when choosing a hat that it should never be wider than your shoulders or it will make you look shorter.

Hats should always give you height and it's a good idea to wear your hat on a slant, rather than flat on your head.

If bold and bright is not your thing, there are plenty of alternatives. Pastel colours and sugared-almond shades are also popular, with soft pinks and lilacs sprinkled around.

This is the time of year to wear florals, lace and pretty pinks, and a lot of clients are going for these pinkie tones as well as powder blue with a hint of silver sparkle.

Whatever you choose, just go for it and have fun.

■ Katherine Elizabeth Millinery, Unit 1.03, Oxo Tower Wharf, Barge House Street, South Bank, London SE1 9PH; 0203 1729768; katherineelizabethhats.com

FASHION

▲ "We love the bold colour-blocking of this dress – it makes a statement while retaining a sense of elegance. The mixture of classic accessories with the contemporary dress really works together"

"Styling dark accessories with this pretty lace dress and the delicate pastel pink hat really adds an edge to this Royal Enclosure look. We saw a lot of beautiful lace ensembles at the royal meeting last season, but this really stood out" ▶

◄ *"We love how this racegoer complements the different use of colour and print with her accessories and her hat. The length of this dress is universally flattering and the detailing of her hat suits the overall look perfectly"*

"Styling black accessories really works for this feminine number. Her matador boater hat and straw circle bag adds an extra dimension to her unique tie-dye print dress. The exaggerated hips is an extremely flattering design detail against the deep-cut neckline and mid-length hem" ►

THE KEY POINTS

Style Guide

ROYAL ENCLOSURE

Ladies
- Dresses and skirts should fall just above the knee or longer
- Dresses and tops should have straps of one inch or greater
- Trouser suits and jumpsuits are welcome – they should be full length, of matching material and colour
- Hats should be worn
- Headpieces must have a solid base of four inches or more

Gentlemen
- Black or grey morning dress must be worn
- With a waistcoat and tie (no cravats)
- A black or grey top hat
- Black shoes with socks

QUEEN ANNE ENCLOSURE

Ladies
- Strapless dresses and tops are not permitted
- A hat, headpiece or fascinator should be worn at all times
- Trousers and jumpsuits must be of full length and shorts are not permitted

Gentlemen
- A suit, shirt and tie must be worn (no bow ties or cravats)
- Jacket and trousers must be of the same colour and pattern
- Socks must be worn

VILLAGE ENCLOSURE

Ladies
- One shoulder dresses, strapless tops and bardot are not permitted
- A hat, headpiece or fascinator should be worn at all times
- Trousers and jumpsuits must be of full length

Gentlemen
- A jacket, full length trousers, collared shirt and tie must be worn
- Jeans, trainers and shorts are not permitted
- Bow ties and cravats are not permitted

WINDSOR ENCLOSURE

Ladies
- Suggestions: Dress for a formal occasion, with a hat or fascinator

Gentlemen
- Suggestions: A jacket, shirt and long trousers should be worn

DO . . .
PLAN AHEAD

Choosing your outfit for the day can be a joy but can also fill many with dread. We advise first-time visitors to sign up to the Royal Ascot newsletter for thorough information on the dress codes and read this year's Style Guide for help with outfit decisions for this year's royal meeting. Take your time, get inspired and enjoy the process.

TRY BEFORE YOU BUY

This is particularly important when choosing your hat. It needs to fit and feel comfortable as it will need to stay secure throughout the day. Play around with different styles and take risks in your choices – you may be surprised at what you thought would suit you and what you thought never could. The same goes for gentlemen: an ill-fitting suit or shoes can cause discomfort throughout the day, so it's important to try them on.

HAVE FUN

Royal Ascot is like nowhere else – it's a day our guests remember forever, so why rush the process? Racegoers should have fun with every step, from choosing what to wear to the big day itself.

DON'T . . .
NEGLECT COMFORT

This is one of the biggest displays of millinery in the world, and so much of the focus is above shoulders, but a lot of time is spent on your feet at Royal Ascot and we strongly advise our guests to consider their footwear choices carefully.

FORGET SOCKS

An addition to this season's dress code is that socks are a requirement for gentlemen in all enclosures.

FORGET TO CHECK THE WEATHER FORECAST

We recommend our guests take practicality into consideration, particularly with the unpredictable British weather. Last year's heatwave was a drastic change from the rain of the previous year, so we advise packing and dressing accordingly.

ALL THE BIGGEST OFFERS
ALL IN ONE PLACE

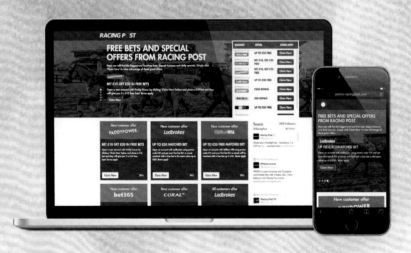

RACINGPOST.COM/FREEBETS

RACING POST

WHEN YOU BET ON ROYAL ASCOT, YOU CAN BET ON RACING POST.

Racing Post backs responsible gambling. 18+ gambleaware.co.uk

DAY FIVE

*T*here was a time when the Saturday of Royal Ascot week was very much the poor relation. They called it Ascot Heath and it was devoid of both Group races and top hats – all Ascot and no Royal, if you like. Then in 2002, to commemorate the Queen's Golden Jubilee, the Saturday was embraced by the rest of the meeting – just for one year, so they said – and it never looked back.

The Group 2 Cork and Orrery Stakes was moved from the Thursday to become the jewel in the crown of the final day, given Group 1 status and renamed the Golden Jubilee Stakes, then ten years later renamed the Diamond Jubilee Stakes, since when it has become an integral part of the Global Sprint Challenge, attracting winners of the calibre of Choisir and Black Caviar, all the way from Australia.

The rise of the six-furlong Diamond Jubilee has mirrored the ascent of the Saturday card to form a thrilling climax to the big week rather than a low-key tailpiece, dominated by speed yet rounded off by the longest Flat race in the entire calendar.

The Queen Alexandra Stakes, run over two miles and six furlongs, was instituted in 1864 and sits as a proud, stamina-sapping anachronism at this glittering meeting, often being plundered by jumps trainers and attracting runners from the first day's two-and-a-half-mile Ascot Handicap, with Simenon the last to complete the double in 2012.

The Saturday begins as usual with the Listed seven-furlong Chesham Stakes for two-year-olds, but then there has been a change to the schedule, with the Group 2 Hardwicke Stakes raised up the order and followed by the Windsor Castle Stakes, which has been moved from the Tuesday with the Wolferton Stakes going in the opposite direction.

The Diamond Jubilee sits as the centrepiece of the card and the speedfest does not end there, as it is followed by the Wokingham Handicap. This is the burn-up to end all burn-ups, a cavalry charge of the top six-furlong handicappers, all looking for precious gaps through which to launch their high-velocity challenges.

The Queen Alexandra may lead us out of the week at a more sedate pace, but it does so as the final event on a card that is now as top-hatted and regal as the rest of the week.

Saturday June 23

RUNNING ORDER

Time / Race	Distance	Prize
2.30 Chesham Stakes (Listed) *Last year's winner: September 11-8f*	**7f** 2yo	£90,000
3.05 Hardwicke Stakes (Group 2) *Last year's winner: Idaho 9-2*	**1m4f** 4yo+	£225,000
3.40 Windsor Castle Stakes (Listed) *Last year's winner: Sound And Silence 16-1*	**5f** 2yo	£90,000
4.20 Diamond Jubilee Stakes (Group 1) *Last year's winner: The Tin Man 9-2*	**6f** 4yo+	£600,000
5.00 Wokingham Stakes (Handicap) *Last year's winner: Out Do 25-1*	**6f** 3yo+	£175,000
5.35 Queen Alexandra Stakes (Conditions) *Last year's winner: Oriental Fox 10-1*	**2m6f** 4yo+	£90,000

Race value is total prize-money

ROYAL ENCLOSURE

This Listed contest is now the first of two races for two-year-olds on the final day, with the Windsor Castle Stakes still to come, and at 7f it is the longest of the week for that age group. It is designed to provide an early stamina test for youngsters, being open only to horses whose sires won over a distance of 1m2f-plus in their own racing careers.

It is no surprise, then, that Aidan O'Brien – the dominant force in Classics both at a mile and over middle distances – has won three times in the last seven years, including the last two runnings with Churchill and September.

He first won the race in 1999 with Bach but then did not strike again until 2011 with Maybe. He is always

Key trends

▶ *By a sire with a stamina index of at least 8.7f, 9/10*
▶ *Raced just once, 8/10 (five had won)*
▶ *Adjusted RPR of at least 91, 8/10*
▶ *Rated within 9lb of RPR top-rated, 7/10*
▶ *Recorded Topspeed figure in excess of 64, 7/10*

Other factors

▶ *Last year, September became the first winner to have previously won over 7f since Bach in 1999 (both trained by Aidan O'Brien)*
▶ *The record of fillies is 2-33*

likely to field a strong candidate nowadays and his ten runners in the past decade have produced three wins, two seconds, a third and a fourth – interestingly, his three winners have come in years when he had just a

single representative (from six runners in total).

The other main trainer to watch is John Gosden, who has had a winner, a runner-up and a third from just six runners in the past decade. Again he has done best in years when he had only a single runner.

Most of the big-priced winners have come in the past decade, with four of the last nine sent off in double figures.

In the longer term, since the distance was raised to 7f in 1996, the majority of winners have been well fancied. Seven of the 22 winners in that period had market leadership, with a further 11 in the top four in the betting.

Most of the winners had raced only once, with 15 of the 22 having won (12 had won their sole start).

Story of the last ten years

	FORM	WINNER		AGE & WGT	Adj RPR	SP	TRAINER	BEST RPR LAST 12 MONTHS (RUNS SINCE)
17	1	**September** D		2 8-12	107T	11-8f	Aidan O'Brien (IRE)	won Leopardstown mdn (7f) (0)
16	3	**Churchill** BF		2 9-3	95-9	8-11f	Aidan O'Brien (IRE)	3rd Curragh mdn (6f) (0)
15	1	**Sunny Way**		2 9-3	91-7	14-1	Eoghan O'Neill (FR)	won Maisons-Laffitte mdn (6f) (0)
14	4	**Richard Pankhurst** BF		2 9-3	87-23	10-1	John Gosden	4th Newmarket Class 4 mdn (6f) (0)
13	3	**Berkshire**		2 9-3	90-11	16-1	Paul Cole	3rd Newbury Class 4 mdn (6f) (0)
12	41	**Tha'ir**		2 9-3	109-1	9-2	Saeed Bin Suroor	won Ripon mdn (6f) (0)
11	1	**Maybe**		2 8-12	109T	5-2f	Aidan O'Brien (IRE)	won Naas mdn (6f) (0)
10	1	**Zaidan**		2 9-3	98-3	7-1	Clive Brittain	won Doncaster Class 5 mdn (5f) (0)
09	42	**Big Audio**		2 9-3	91-12	22-1	Richard Hannon Snr	2nd Doncaster Class 5 mdn (6f) (0)
08	1	**Free Agent**		2 9-3	98T	7-2j	Richard Hannon Snr	won Leicester Class 4 mdn (6f) (0)

FAVOURITES £-0.37

TRAINERS IN THIS RACE (w-pl-r) Aidan O'Brien 3-3-10, John Gosden 1-2-6, Paul Cole 1-0-3, Charlie Hills 0-0-2, Eve Johnson Houghton 0-0-2, James Tate 0-0-2, Mark Johnston 0-2-12, Michael Bell 0-0-2, Richard Hannon 0-0-4, Simon Crisford 0-0-2

FATE OF FAVOURITES 1201423211 **POSITION OF WINNER IN MARKET** 1041384611

BESPOKE SHOOTING OPPORTUNITIES ON SOME OF THE UK'S MOST PRESTIGIOUS ESTATES

OVER 50 YEARS EXPERIENCE IN THE GAME SHOOTING FIELD

BOOK A FULL TEAM OR JOIN OUR ROVING SYNDICATE AS A SINGLE GUN

VIEW AVAILABILITY ONLINE **WWW.IANCOLEY.CO.UK/SPORTING-AGENCY** OR CALL TODAY **01242 870391**

01242 870391
www.IANCOLEY.co.uk
Nr. Andoversford · Cheltenham · GL54 4AX

IAN COLEY

GUNSHOP • SHOOTING SCHOOL
SPORTING AGENCY • COUNTRY CLOTHING

This Group 2 race over 1m4f is for four-year-olds and upwards and often provides a showcase for horses who were in the Derby picture the previous year – and sometimes signals the blossoming of a high-class talent who will go on to greater achievements.

The last ten winners were all four-year-olds and they had followed similar career paths to this point, with eight of them having competed the previous year in at least one of the St Leger, the Great Voltigeur Stakes at York or the King Edward VII Stakes at Royal Ascot.

The Great Voltigeur appears most commonly in their records – three won at York, two were runner-up and two were unplaced. The previous year's result of that contest is always a good starting point for this race.

Two of the four who had run in the previous year's St Leger had finished third, while 2017 scorer Idaho unseated at Doncaster but had previously been third in the Derby and second in the Irish Derby. One of the three who had run in the King Edward VII had won, with the other two unplaced.

As for current-season form, the Coronation Cup at Epsom, the Gordon Richards Stakes at Sandown and middle-distance races at Chester are key staging posts.

This is Sir Michael Stoute's best race at Royal Ascot with ten winners, seven of them in the last 12 runnings. Aidan O'Brien has had three winners, all in the past decade, and the only other current trainer to have won since 2006 is John Gosden

with Bronze Cannon in 2009.

Mark Johnston has had four winners, although the most recent of them was Bandari in 2005.

Key trends
▸ *Aged four, 10/10*
▸ *Group-race winner, 10/10*
▸ *Won over at least 1m4f, 10/10*
▸ *Adjusted RPR of at least 129, 9/10*
▸ *Finished in first three in a Listed or Group race that season, 9/10*

Other factors
▸ *Five favourites have won in the past decade*
▸ *Ormonde Stakes winners have finished 5110517*
▸ *Four of Sir Michael Stoute's last five winners had run at Chester that season*
▸ *Two of Aidan O'Brien's three winners ran in Epsom's Coronation Cup (36)*

Story of the last ten years

FORM		WINNER	AGE & WGT	Adj RPR	SP	TRAINER	BEST RPR LAST 12 MONTHS (RUNS SINCE)
17	1U5-6	Idaho D	4 9-1	133⁻¹	9-2	Aidan O'Brien (IRE)	2nd Irish Derby Gp1 (1m4f) (4)
16	53-11	Dartmouth CD	4 9-1	129⁻⁷	10-1	Sir Michael Stoute	won Ormonde Stakes Gp3 (1m5½f) (0)
15	237-1	Snow Sky D	4 9-1	130⁻⁸	12-1	Sir Michael Stoute	won Yorkshire Cup Gp2 (1m6f) (0)
14	21-22	Telescope D	4 9-1	130ᵀ	7-4f	Sir Michael Stoute	2nd Huxley Stakes Gp3 (1m2½f) (0)
13	58-22	Thomas Chippendale CD	4 9-0	129⁻⁶	8-1	Lady Cecil	won King Edward VII Stakes Gp2 (1m4f) (4)
12	132-1	Sea Moon D	4 9-0	139ᵀ	3-1f	Sir Michael Stoute	won Great Voltigeur Stakes Gp2 (1m4f) (3)
11	/11-1	Await The Dawn	4 9-0	139ᵀ	4-6f	Aidan O'Brien (IRE)	won Huxley Stakes Gp3 (1m2½f) (0)
10	73-11	Harbinger D	4 9-0	140ᵀ	8-11f	Sir Michael Stoute	won Ormonde Stakes Gp3 (1m5½f) (0)
09	5-331	Bronze Cannon D	4 9-3	127⁻⁵	8-1	John Gosden	won Jockey Club Stakes Gp2 (1m4f) (0)
08	6-713	Macarthur	4 9-0	136ᵀ	11-8f	Aidan O'Brien (IRE)	3rd Coronation Cup Gp1 (1m4f) (0)

WINS-RUNS 4yo 10-8-55, 5yo 0-5-17, 6yo+ 0-6-24 **FAVOURITES** £2.52

TRAINERS IN THIS RACE (w-pl-r) Sir Michael Stoute 5-2-18, Aidan O'Brien 3-1-6, John Gosden 1-2-8, Clive Cox 0-0-1, Ralph Beckett 0-1-2, Roger Varian 0-1-5, Saeed Bin Suroor 0-1-10, William Haggas 0-1-3

FATE OF FAVOURITES 1211151604 **POSITION OF WINNER IN MARKET** 1311141462

Moorcroft
Racehorse Welfare Centre

PROVIDING THE
VERY BEST FOR CARE
FOR OUR WONDERFUL
HORSES AWAITING A NEW
HOME AND A NEW LIFE

This centre in the south of England was set up to ensure that retired racehorses whatever age, can be re-trained to find another career in life. Much care and attention is given to each individual horse and when fully retrained new homes are found. The centre retains ownership for life and visits these horses every year to ensure that all is well.

This charity depends on generous donations from horse lovers. Many horses need a time for rehabilitation due to injury etc and start to enjoy an easier life after their racing careers. Visits by appointment are welcomed. Please ring Mary Frances, Manager, on 07929 666408 for more information or to arrange a visit.

Huntingrove Stud, Slinfold, West Sussex. RH13 0RB
Tel: 07929 666408 | Email: moorcroftracehorse@gmail.com | www.moorcroftracehorse.org.uk

This Listed race over 5f is now the final race of the week for two-year-olds, having been switched from its previous Tuesday slot to allow the Wolferton Stakes to make the reverse move.

In recent years this has proved the juvenile race most open to a surprise result, with seven of the last 12 winners having been priced at 14-1 or bigger. Perhaps the less high-profile stables save their best hopes for this contest, knowing that the big guns will aim their main fire at the more important juvenile races.

It is notable that eight trainers have achieved their first Royal Ascot success in the last 20 runnings of this contest, including Jamie Osborne and Michael Bell. However, even the major

Key trends

▶ *Top-four finish last time out, 10/10 (five won)*

▶ *Lost maiden tag, 9/10*

▶ *By a sire with a stamina index of 6.5f-8f, 9/10*

▶ *Ran two or three times, 7/10 (all three exceptions were once-raced winners)*

▶ *Adjusted RPR of at least 94, 8/10 (one exception was unrated)*

Other factors

▶ *Only one winner had scored outside maiden/novice company (Frederick Engels in 2011)*

▶ *Fillies won five editions in a row between 1996 and 2000 but only two have been placed in the last ten years*

▶ *The race is often won by trainers not usually associated with having Royal Ascot winners*

stables can produce a long-odds winner – Charlie Appleby at 16-1 last year and John Gosden at 20-1 the year before – and just four of the last ten winners were in the top six in the betting.

Aidan O'Brien's only success came with Washington DC in 2015 and this is a race that usually goes to a British-trained runner, although US trainer Wesley Ward has broken the mould twice with Strike The Tiger in 2009 (his breakthrough year at Royal Ascot) and Hootenanny in 2014.

Most winners had shown a decent level of form. The last nine had lost their maiden tag and the three once-raced winners in that period had all been successful, while three of the last four winners had already been tried in Listed company.

Story of the last ten years

FORM		WINNER	AGE & WGT	Adj RPR	SP	TRAINER	BEST RPR LAST 12 MONTHS (RUNS SINCE)
17	14	**Sound And Silence** D	2 9-3	101⁻¹¹	16-1	Charlie Appleby	4th Sandown Listed (5f) (0)
16	1	**Ardad** D	2 9-3	94⁻¹⁴	20-1	John Gosden	won Yarmouth Class 4 (5f) (0)
15	212	**Washington DC** D, BF	2 9-3	106⁻²	5-1	Aidan O'Brien (IRE)	2nd Curragh Listed (5f) (0)
14	13	**Hootenanny** BF	2 9-3	95⁻¹³	7-2f	Wesley Ward (USA)	3rd Pimlico Listed (5f) (0)
13	14	**Extortionist** D	2 9-3	98⁻¹⁰	16-1	Olly Stevens	won Nottingham Class 5 mdn (5f) (1)
12	321	**Hototo** D	2 9-3	100⁻⁸	14-1	Kevin Ryan	won Ayr Class 4 mdn (5f) (0)
11	221	**Frederick Engels** D	2 9-3	114ᵀ	9-4f	David Brown	won Musselburgh Class 2 (5f) (0)
10	1	**Marine Commando** D	2 9-3	105⁻⁶	9-2	Richard Fahey	won Carlisle Class 5 auct mdn (5f) (0)
09	1	**Strike The Tiger**	2 9-3	-	33-1	Wesley Ward (USA)	won Churchill Downs mdn (4½f) (0)
08	33	**Flashmans Paper**	2 9-3	85⁻²⁹	100-1	John Best	3rd Windsor Class 5 mdn (5f) (1)

FAVOURITES -£2.25

TRAINERS IN THIS RACE (w-pl-r) Wesley Ward 2-0-9, Aidan O'Brien 1-2-7, Richard Fahey 1-1-8, Charlie Appleby 1-1-3, David Evans 0-0-7, David O'Meara 0-1-3, George Margarson 0-0-2, Stan Moore 0-0-8, Richard Hannon 0-0-8, Roger Varian 0-0-4, Tom Dascombe 0-0-7, Bryan Smart 0-0-2

FATE OF FAVOURITES 2001031300 **POSITION OF WINNER IN MARKET** 0021791207

This is the big 6f sprint of the week for older horses (open only to four-year-olds and upwards since the advent of the Commonwealth Cup for three-year-olds).

Connections usually choose between this race and the King's Stand over 5f on the Tuesday but sometimes runners contest both races and Australian raider Choisir completed the double in 2003.

Since the race was upgraded to Group 1 in 2002 there have been 16 winners and half of them were priced in double figures, with only three successful favourites.

However, even most of the longer-priced winners brought a strong level of form, with 12 of the 16 having been placed at least in a Group 1 in the previous 12 months (seven had won), and the other four at least having competed at that level.

Generally the longer-priced winners have come from the group who had been placed in a Group 1 but not yet won at that level. The main races to check for that type of horse are the previous year's running of this race, the July Cup and Haydock Sprint Cup.

The British Champions Sprint, run over course and distance the previous October, is fast developing into a key guide. The last three British or Irish winners had run there, finishing 121.

The best prep race has been the Duke of York Stakes, with five of the ten British-trained winners since 2002 having run there for finishing positions of 03255 (Aidan O'Brien's Starspangledbanner also prepped there in 2010, finishing fifth).

One explanation for the step up in performance from the Duke of York (and the fact that only four of the last 16 winners had scored on their previous outing) is that the ground often changes from May to June.

Last year The Tin Man was fifth in the Duke of York on soft (a surface he has never won on) but the going was good to firm for the Diamond Jubilee five weeks later (he had won three times

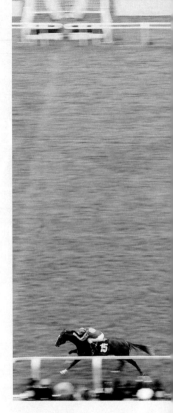

before in such conditions).

Twelve of the last 16 runnings have been contested on good to firm (or firm) and ten of the dozen winners in those years had already won on that kind of surface.

4.20 Diamond Jubilee Stakes

Key trends
▶ *No older than six, 10/10*
▶ *Adjusted RPR of at least 125, 9/10*
▶ *Group or Listed winner over 6f, 8/10*
▶ *Trained in Britain or Ireland, 8/10*
▶ *Ran at a previous Royal Ascot, 6/10 (one won, two placed and three unplaced)*

Other factors
▶ *Only three winners had scored earlier in the season*
▶ *One winner was unplaced in the King's Stand that week*
▶ *Three winners had run in the race the year before, finishing 278*
▶ *Four winners contested the Duke of York Stakes, in which they finished 5255. Duke of York winners finished 092942*

Starspangledbanner scores in 2010, while The Tin Man (opposite page) leads them home last year

DIAMOND JUBILEE STAKES

INTERNATIONAL WINNERS

Choisir (2003)

The first Australian-trained horse to triumph in Britain, landing both the King's Stand Stakes and the Diamond Jubilee Stakes (then the Golden Jubilee); the first horse to complete the Royal Ascot sprint double since Diadem in 1920

Cape Of Good Hope (2005)

The first Hong Kong-trained horse to win in Britain, scoring for ex-pat Englishman David Oughton in the year the royal meeting was transferred to York

Black Caviar (2012)

One of the best sprinters of all time and unbeaten in 25 starts in a glittering career. The Australian-trained mare scored at odds of 1-6 at Royal Ascot, despite jockey Luke Nolen almost snatching defeat from the jaws of victory by easing up near the line

Undrafted (2015)

The first US-trained winner of this prize, scoring at 14-1 for Royal Ascot regular Wesley Ward and jockey Frankie Dettori

BETTING

Longest-priced winner: Kearney 40-1 (1980)

Shortest-priced winner: Black Caviar 1-6 (2012)

Market leaders: 24 favourites or joint favourites have been successful in 72 runnings

* All figures since 1946

WINNING CONNECTIONS

Most successful trainer
5 wins: Vincent O'Brien

Welsh Saint (1970)
Saritamer (1974)
Swingtime (1975)
Thatching (1979)
College Chapel (1993)

Most successful jockey
9 wins: Lester Piggott

Right Boy (1958, 1959)
Tin Whistle (1960)
El Gallo (1963)
Mountain Call (1968)
Welsh Saint (1970)
Saritamer (1974)
Thatching (1979)
College Chapel (1993)

Most successful owners
2 wins: Giles Loder
Abadan (1950), Blood Test (1953)

Stanhope Joel
Matador (1957), Bun Penny (1961)

Geoffrey Gilbert
Right Boy (1958, 1959)

Charles St George
El Gallo (1963), Saritamer (1974)

Robert Sangster
Thatching (1979), Committed (1984)

Maktoum Al Maktoum
Great Commotion (1990), Royal Applause (1997)

Hamdan Al Maktoum
Atraf (1996), Malhub (2002)

Hamdan Al Maktoum

This is one of the big handicap sprints, with close on 30 runners charging down the straight in a hotly contested 6f race.

Many will focus on the draw but recent runnings suggest the winner can come from anywhere on the track. Last year victory went to the lowest-drawn runner, Out Do in stall one, but the fourth-placed runner came from the opposite side in stall 31 and there was less than a length between them (two of the first four came from the lowest six numbers and the other two from the highest four).

Even though only one favourite has won since 2005, seven of the 12 winners since then have come from the first four in the market.

Winners have tended to come from a narrow weights range, from 8st 12lb to 9st

DID YOU KNOW?

Ascot is famed for being a tough course, with a 73ft climb from the lowest point (Swinley Bottom) to the highest (winning post). Grass is cut to a regulation 4in for Flat racing

Key trends

▶ *Distance winner, 10/10*
▶ *Within 7lb of RPR top-rated 10/10*
▶ *Officially rated between 95 and 106, 10/10*
▶ *Carried no more than 9st 3lb, 9/10*
▶ *Aged four or five, 8/10*
▶ *No more than four runs that season, 8/10*
▶ *Top-four finish last time out, 8/10*
▶ *Won over 7f, 7/10*
▶ *Won in Class 1 or 2, 6/10*

Other factors

▶ *Three winners were drawn between 12 and 22, four in one to 11 and three between 23 and 31*
▶ *Five winners were top or joint top-rated*

3lb. Last year four of the first five carried 8st 13lb to 9st 1lb (taking into account riders' claims) and the previous year the first three carried 9st 1lb or 9st 2lb.

The importance of getting into the race on the right sort of handicap mark is evident in the fact that only two of the last 12 winners had won that season, although nine had achieved a top-four finish last time out. Seven had gone up in the handicap that season (only three had dropped), so it is important to have shown a good level of form.

Big-field experience is also important, with eight of the last 12 winners having won or been placed in a field of 18 runners or more.

Newmarket stables have the best long-term record but northern-based trainers have done well recently, winning three of the last five runnings.

	FORM	WINNER	AGE	& WGT	OR	SP	TRAINER	BEST RPR LAST 12 MONTHS (RUNS SINCE)
17	7-304	**Out Do** D	8	8-13	99⁻²	25-1	David O'Meara	3rd Ascot Class 2 hcap (5f) (7)
16	40-70	**Outback Traveller** C, D	5	9-1	100ᵀ	10-1	Robert Cowell	4th Ascot Class 2 hcap (7f) (3)
15	413-2	**Interception** D	5	9-3	102⁻⁶	10-1	David Lanigan	2nd Haydock Listed (6f) (0)
14	50-22	**Baccarat** D, BF	5	9-2	105ᵀ	9-1	Richard Fahey	2nd York Class 2 hcap (6f) (0)
13	56142	**York Glory** D	5	9-2	100ᵀ	14-1	Kevin Ryan	2nd York Class 2 hcap (5f) (0)
12	-5992	**Dandy Boy** C, D	6	9-8	106⁻⁷	33-1	David Marnane (IRE)	2nd Curragh hcap (1m) (0)
11	230-2	**Deacon Blues** D	4	8-13	98⁻¹	15-2	James Fanshawe	2nd Ascot Class 3 hcap (6f) (0)
10	1316/	**Laddies Poker Two** CD, BF	5	8-11	95ᵀ	9-2f	Jeremy Noseda	Seasonal debut (0)
09	22-11	**High Standing** (5ex) D	4	8-12	96ᵀ	6-1	William Haggas	won Goodwood Class 2 hcap (6f) (0)
08	82202	**Big Timer** D	4	9-2	100⁻¹	20-1	Linda Perratt	2nd Haydock Gp3 (7f) (0)

WINS-RUNS 3yo 0-0-1, 4yo 3-10-91, 5yo 5-7-65, 6yo+ 2-13-110 **FAVOURITES** -£4.50

FATE OF FAVOURITES 0010000528 **POSITION OF WINNER IN MARKET** 0212064440

5.35 Queen Alexandra Stakes

This is the longest race of the week at two and three-quarter miles – indeed, the longest run under Flat racing rules – and one of the best loved, with just one of its traditional aspects being that it always closes the meeting.

With fewer out-and-out stayers in Flat yards nowadays, this race is more open to being won by a trainer better known for jump racing. Nicky Henderson and Willie Mullins (twice) – the current British and Irish champion jumps trainers – figure on the roll of honour in the past nine years (as they do in other staying races at the meeting), along with Mullins' great Irish rival Gordon Elliott and Gary Moore.

Four of the five winners

Key trends
▶ *Officially rated 90-plus, 10/10*
▶ *Drawn nine or higher, 9/10*
▶ *Aged four to seven, 8/10*
▶ *Adjusted RPR at least 113, 8/10 (exceptions hurdlers)*
▶ *Contested a Group or Listed race since last season, 8/10*
▶ *Rated within 7lb of RPR top-rated, 7/10*
▶ *Top-six finish in race over 2m2f-plus, 6/10*

Other factors
▶ *Only two winners had scored that season*

from those yards had been running over jumps during the winter and each one of that quartet had run at one of the big spring jumps festivals at Cheltenham, Aintree and Punchestown.

Swingkeel, the 2011 winner, had been tried unsuccessfully over hurdles

in the winter with Nigel Twiston-Davies before returning to John Dunlop to win this race.

Mullins has the best record with figures of 08114032 since 2010 (25%, +3pt). He did the Ascot Handicap/ Queen Alexandra double with Simenon at the 2012 meeting and went close last year when Thomas Hobson won the first leg but was beaten into second here. Baddam also did the double in 2006 for Mick Channon.

Aidan O'Brien won in 2008 with Honolulu and his only two runners since then have been placed.

Most winners are prominent in the market, with seven of the last ten winners coming from the first four in the betting and nothing bigger than Commissioned (12-1 in 2016) since 2004.

Story of the last ten years

FORM	WINNER		AGE & WGT	Adj RPR	SP	TRAINER	BEST RPR LAST 12 MONTHS (RUNS SINCE)
17	95-25	Oriental Fox CD	9 9-5	117-10	10-1	Mark Johnston	2nd Newmarket Class 2 hcap (1m6f) (1)
16	211/	Commissioned	6 9-2	113-11	12-1	Gordon Elliott (IRE)	Seasonal debut (0)
15	3756-	Oriental Fox	7 9-2	120-1	4-1	Mark Johnston	6th Northumberland Plate hcap (2m) (0)
14	321-5	Pique Sous	7 9-2	108-18	11-4	Willie Mullins (IRE)	won Leopardstown hcap (1m6f) (1)
13	525-5	Chiberta King	7 9-2	119T	8-1	Andrew Balding	5th Goodwood Gp2 (2m) (3)
12	350-1	Simenon C	5 9-2	119-7	11-4f	Willie Mullins (IRE)	won Ascot Class 2 hcap (2m4f) (0)
11	30-06	Swingkeel	6 9-2	113-5	11-2	John Dunlop	3rd Salisbury Class 2 (1m6f) (3)
10	112/5	Bergo	7 9-2	106-6	10-1	Gary Moore	5th Newbury Class 1 Listed (1m5½f) (0)
09	541-1	Caracciola	12 9-7	116T	6-1	Nicky Henderson	won Cesarewitch Handicap (2m2f) (1)
08	338-4	Honolulu BF	4 9-5	126T	7-4f	Aidan O'Brien (IRE)	2nd Ebor Handicap (1m6f) (4)

WINS-RUNS: 4yo 1-8-36, 5yo 1-2-28, 6yo+ 8-10-91 **FAVOURITES:** -£3.50

TRAINERS IN THIS RACE (w-pl-r) Willie Mullins 2-2-8, Aidan O'Brien 1-2-3, Mark Johnston 2-0-4, Andrew Balding 1-0-4, Alan King 0-0-4, Charlie Appleby 0-0-2, Mick Channon 0-0-2, Hughie Morrison 0-0-2

FATE OF FAVOURITES 1462124432 **POSITION OF WINNER IN MARKET** 1552142364

FIVE OF THE BEST ...

TUESDAY

The Lockinge is the key pointer for the Queen Anne Stakes and one ploy is to side with something that finished outside the first three at Newbury and whose SP is lower than 20-1 at Ascot. Since 1998 the system would have returned five winners from 19 qualifiers at prices ranging from 100-30 to 12-1 (26%, +20.33pt). It would also have returned six placed horses at prices ranging from 9-1 to 16-1.

WEDNESDAY

In the past decade Guineas form has become important in the Jersey Stakes, with seven of the last ten winners having run in one of the European early-season Classics. Since 2008 there have been 40 qualifiers at an 18 per cent strike-rate with a level-stake profit of +31pt.

THURSDAY

Since 1998 13 horses who were beaten in York's Dante in May lined up in the Hampton Court Stakes, with five winning at prices of 9-2, 8-1, 8-1, 20-1 and 33-1 (38%, +65.50pt). Later on the card, the Britannia can be one of the toughest races for punters but it pays to concentrate on runners at single-figure odds who fulfil three criteria – officially rated 87 to 96; carrying less than 9st 2lb; top-three finish within last two starts. In the past ten years there have been four winners from 20 qualifiers (20%, +13.50pt).

Key trends

FRIDAY

A common theme among King Edward VII Stakes victors is Newmarket form, as 15 of the 20 winners since 1998 had previously run on the Rowley Mile. As the race doesn't provide many upsets, the best ploy is to concentrate on single-figure-priced runners, and backing those less than 10-1 with Newmarket form would have found the 15 winners from 55 qualifiers. (27%, +28.75pt).

SATURDAY

Sometimes it pays to keep it simple and that is certainly true when looking at the Chesham, with once-raced winners more than paying their way. Of the 256 runners in the last 20 runnings of the 7f Listed contest for juveniles, 49 have had such a profile with 11 of those obliging, including September last year. The system strikes at 22 per cent, providing a level-stake profit of +25.25pt.

Permian lands last season's Dante from Benbatl, who went on to win the Hampton Court Stakes the following month; (right) September comes home clear to win the 2017 Chesham Stakes

FIVE OF THE BEST . . .

Racing Post photographer
Edward Whitaker picks the
perfect picture locations

▲ The charm and colour of the bandstand

▲ The bronze statues of the
royal family meeting their
workers, near the old winner's
enclosure gates on the edge of
the Royal Enclosure lawn

The back of the
parade ring with
the grandstand as a
backdrop (particularly
when it's sunny) ▶

Photo opportunities

◄ Get a good position by the running rails to snap the royal procession coming up the course

The gates in front of the new stand from the High Street side ►

THE DRAW

Racing Post experts Graeme Rodway, Tom Segal and James Pyman give their views on this vital talking point

HOW MUCH IMPORTANCE DO YOU ATTACH TO THE DRAW AT ROYAL ASCOT?

Graeme Rodway It's a factor but not a major one. Ability, going, form at the distance, course and trainer form are all probably more important. A decent jockey helps too.

Tom Segal It's a massive factor but it's impossible to predict, so it's way down my list. Ability is by far the most important consideration. My way into Ascot races is to concentrate on hold-up horses, jockeys (Jamie Spencer specifically) and sires. The ground is different from everywhere else and certain sires like Exceed And Excel do well there.

Expert analysis

James Pyman It's something I always consider in races on the round course – it helps piece together the likely early positions of the runners. On the straight course the significance of the draw varies depending on evidence from earlier results. When there is a strong pattern I take heed. However, pace is a more important factor when studying straight-course races.

WHAT ARE THE IMPORTANT DRAW FACTORS?

Graeme Rodway It's hard to say as the effect of the draw can vary day by day and that would suggest there's not a lot in it. One day the far side can be favoured and most race that side, then the following day that ground has been cut up and the stands side is the place to be. It's probably fair all the way

across. I don't like being drawn on either wing.

Tom Segal The draw bias will change from day to day, even from race to race, so it's not worth considering and the nonsense talked about pace amuses me. If we could guarantee how each horse was going to run we could maybe make a guess on pace bias but that's too tricky, especially if the jockeys think there is an advantage on one side or the other. ▶

James Pyman When field sizes are bigger, low-drawn horses can be at an advantage on the round course, particularly over a mile. I don't have a strong opinion with regards to any general advantage on the straight course. It can vary from meeting to meeting, even from day to day, and can be affected by going and the mindsets of the jockeys. Often when one or two results point to one side riding quicker, jockeys will make a beeline for that part of the track and consequently that is often where the majority of the pace is. Another consideration when assessing pace is runners' typical running styles.

DO GROUND CONDITIONS MAKE A DIFFERENCE?

Graeme Rodway Low numbers did well on soft ground last year but, looking at the stats over a longer period, there doesn't appear a lot in it whatever the going.

Tom Segal Soft ground is likely to cause track biases but at Ascot it changes constantly.

James Pyman When it's soft on the round course I don't expect there to be any significant draw advantage and instead I would focus on horses who will act on the ground. The fields tend to be really big at Royal Ascot on the straight course and there aren't many past examples of such races, meaning we're mostly in the dark with regards to draw bias if the ground gets soft, although often in these conditions the runners race as one group.

IN BIG FIELDS ON THE STRAIGHT COURSE, IS IT A GOOD TACTIC TO BACK A HORSE ON EACH SIDE?

Graeme Rodway It depends if you fancy a horse on both sides. I wouldn't set out with the intention of doing so. If I fancied a horse on each side I would do it, but if I fancied two on one side and none on the other I wouldn't back one on each side.

Tom Segal It's always a good idea to back a couple in big-field races but I would be more inclined to back the two horses I consider to be the fastest than worry too much about the draw, which is only guesswork these days.

James Pyman Yes, it's a tactic I deploy regularly. There is nothing worse than seeing the horse you have backed finish first on the 'wrong' side in a race won by another runner high on your shortlist.

HOW MUCH NOTICE DO YOU TAKE IF EARLY RESULTS AT THE MEETING SUGGEST A DRAW BIAS?

Graeme Rodway Given it can vary from day to day, I definitely take an interest in which side has prevailed in the earlier races on that day. The main reason for this is the jockeys take note too and often congregate towards the favoured side, so if you're already drawn on that side you have an advantage.

Tom Segal If there appears to be a bias the jockeys will tend to gravitate towards it. I would watch Jamie Spencer because he's a maverick in these big-field handicaps and will know where the runners are going to congregate.

James Pyman Any apparent bias in previous races must be factored in, primarily because it influences riding tactics/pace. However, bookmakers take note too, shortening perceived well-drawn horses and lengthening others. Just when you think you have a handle on the straight course it has a habit of throwing up an unexpected result. I will still back a horse earlier results suggest is berthed on the 'wrong' side if the price looks big enough.

EFFECT OF DRAW AT ROYAL ASCOT

Straight-course races with 16+ runners (2013-17)

Top 4 finishers shown by draw section

■ Low　　Middle　　■ High

2013

Winners from each section: H7 M1 L3

Race	Distance	Going	1st	2nd	3rd	4th
King's Stand	5f	Good	H	L	M	L
Windsor Castle	5f	Good	H	H	H	M
Jersey	7f	GF	L	M	H	L
Queen Mary	5f	GF	H	L	L	L
Royal Hunt Cup	1m	GF	L	L	M	L
Sandringham	1m	GF	L	L	L	H
Britannia	1m	GF	M	M	H	H
Albany	6f	GF	H	H	M	H
Chesham	7f	GF	H	M	M	L
Diamond Jubilee	6f	GF	H	M	H	L
Wokingham	6f	GF	H	H	M	H

2014

Winners from each section: H7 M2 L0

Race	Distance	Going	1st	2nd	3rd	4th
King's Stand	5f	Good	M	L	M	M
Windsor Castle	5f	Good	H	H	H	L
Jersey	7f	GF	H	L	M	H
Queen Mary	5f	GF	M	H	H	M
Royal Hunt Cup	1m	GF	H	M	H	H
Sandringham	1m	GF	H	H	H	H
Britannia	1m	GF	H	H	M	H
Albany	6f	GF	H	M	M	M
Wokingham	6f	GF	H	M	M	H

2015

Winners from each section: H4 M5 L2

Race	Distance	Going	1st	2nd	3rd	4th
Coventry	6f	GF	M	M	L	M
King's Stand	5f	GF	L	L	M	H
Windsor Castle	5f	GF	L	L	M	L
Jersey	7f	GF	M	M	L	M
Queen Mary	5f	GF	H	L	L	H
Royal Hunt Cup	1m	GF	M	M	L	H
Sandringham	1m	GF	H	L	L	M
Britannia	1m	GF	M	L	H	L
Albany	6f	GF	H	H	M	M
Commonwealth Cup	6f	GF	M	H	M	L
Wokingham	6f	GF	H	H	L	M

2016

Winners from each section: H5 M3 L2

Race	Distance	Going	1st	2nd	3rd	4th
Coventry	6f	Soft	H	L	M	L
King's Stand	5f	Soft	M	H	M	H
Windsor Castle	5f	Soft	L	L	M	H
Jersey	7f	Soft	M	H	L	L
Queen Mary	5f	Soft	H	M	L	M
Royal Hunt Cup	1m	Soft	L	H	H	M
Sandringham	1m	Soft	H	H	H	M
Britannia	1m	Soft	M	H	H	H
Albany	6f	GS	H	L	H	H
Wokingham	6f	GS	H	M	H	L

2017

Winners from each section: H3 M5 L5

Race	Distance	Going	1st	2nd	3rd	4th
Coventry	6f	GF	M	H	L	M
King's Stand	5f	GF	H	L	M	L
Queen Anne	1m	GF	L	M	M	H
Windsor Castle	5f	GF	M	L	L	M
Jersey	7f	GF	M	H	H	H
Queen Mary	5f	GF	H	H	H	M
Royal Hunt Cup	1m	GF	H	H	M	M
Sandringham	1m	GF	M	H	H	M
Britannia	1m	GF	L	L	L	H
Norfolk	5f	GF	L	H	H	L
Albany	6f	GF	M	L	H	H
Diamond Jubilee	6f	GF	L	M	H	M
Wokingham	6f	GF	L	L	M	M

HANDICAPS

Dave Orton on the key factors
to assess in the handicap races

DRAW

The draw can be an important factor even in the long-distance handicaps. In the 2m4f Ascot Handicap, for example, those berthed high have held an advantage over the years. Largely that's due to a prolonged run into the first turn that often results in rough starts for those racing nearer the rail. Last year's first three in an 18-runner field came from stalls 11, 17 and 10.

In handicaps over shorter distances on the round course, however, it's a definite help to save ground by not being drawn wide. Runners who get too far back in the pack are disadvantaged, as the races become really serious nearing the final bend and it's not easy to mow down a large number of rivals in the short home straight.

Looking for a prominent racer drawn low to middle is a sensible approach in the shorter round-course handicaps.

PACE

On the straight track it's more recently become a matter of where the pace lies, and that's something punters have to map out for themselves. For years there was a perceived draw bias suiting those nearer the stands and exotic bets featuring runners starting from high numbers often paid out handsomely. However, mainly due to more consistent overnight watering by course officials during a dry week, it's amazing how quickly any draw bias can be wiped out the next day.

On Wednesday last year it paid to race nearside in the 1m Royal Hunt Cup, with Zhui Feng making all from stall 26, while in the closing Sandringham

Nearside was the place to be in last year's Royal Hunt Cup, while backing runners trained by Willie Mullins (below) in the Ascot Stakes has paid well in recent years with three of the last six winners

Handicap the stands side was also the place to be. However, the following day the first three home in the Britannia Handicap, run over the same course and distance, all raced on the far side (low numbers). Identifying probable front-runners in advance is a must.

FORM

Previous course form can be important in the handicaps for older horses and don't discount all-weather specialists either, as the Ascot track has sand-based turf.

Four of last year's eight handicap winners had run on the all-weather that season and/or won on that surface, while two of the five winners in handicaps open to older horses had strong course form.

It's hard to knock winning form, but simply relying on that in handicaps has proved a costly exercise for punters. The record of last-time-out winners since 2015 is 8/128 (6%) for a level-stake loss of -69.50pt. In 2017 that statistic hit an all-time low of 0-39 runners failing to follow up a previous success. Ten of those losers were from the top three in the betting too, so looking away from the obvious form horses often results in some value.

TRAINERS

Everyone has their favourite trainers, of course. Aidan O'Brien doesn't have too many handicap starters but is 2/9 at the past three meetings for a +10pt profit to level stakes. The one who really sticks out in that time is John Gosden, though. The Newmarket maestro is 3/23 in handicaps, with three placing last year at odds of 14-1, 20-1 and 66-1. That makes the point that second or third strings from the big stables are well worth a second look.

In the Ascot Handicap over its marathon journey of 2m4f, the first port of call for backers should be runners from top jumps stables who already have form on the Flat. Since Tony Martin's Barba Papa landed a gamble in 2000, a staggering 13 renewals have gone to jumps trainers. Irish horses have taken five of the last six runnings, with champion trainer Willie Mullins *(left)* responsible for three of them.

117

HORSES TO WATCH

Racing Post experts each give a top tip for the meeting

Pietro Innocenzi

EMARAATY
Commonwealth Cup

Despite the fact he has raced exclusively over 7f and has a pedigree that suggests he needs at least a mile, I've been dying to see the headstrong Emaraaty tried over sprint trips and John Gosden's three-year-old wouldn't be the first winner of this race to be dropping in distance (significantly, the two big-race entries he has held all spring are for this and the 6f July Cup). He has a boom-or-bust profile, having flopped when stepped up in class in last season's Dewhurst, but the fact connections felt he was up to it on the back of a Newbury novice win speaks volumes and he looks the sort who will thrive in a strongly run race on decent ground.

Graeme Rodway

GHOSTWATCH
Queen's Vase

This Godolphin three-year-old never went a yard when sent off a heavily backed favourite at Chester's May meeting but stayed on powerfully

and did well to finish third as he wasn't suited by the turning track. A strong-galloping type who needs a stiffer course and test of stamina, the Charlie Appleby-trained colt will be suited by a step up in distance and looks the sort who could go well in the Queen's Vase, for which he holds an entry.

Justin O'Hanlon

US NAVY FLAG
Jersey Stakes

Last season's champion juvenile has had an eventful campaign so far and almost came down in the French 2,000 Guineas while running very creditably. That run should finally hammer home that he doesn't get a mile under the front-running tactics that have been employed so successfully over shorter trips. He could run in the Commonwealth Cup but

the Jersey Stakes over 7f before going sprinting is just as likely. It is the route that Mozart took years ago in becoming champion sprinter and this horse could well be in the same mould.

Tom Segal

SIOUX NATION
Commonwealth Cup

The Ascot surface seems to play into the hands of American sires like Scat Daddy and I can see his son Sioux Nation following up last year's Norfolk Stakes win in the Commonwealth Cup. He went on to win in Group 1 company at the Curragh and his whole season is being tailored around the royal meeting. The Commonwealth Cup looks a much weaker race than it has been and Sioux Nation could easily be a class apart.

Emaraaty could prove a potent force in the Commonwealth Cup

Crystal Ocean is fancied for success in the Group 2 Hardwicke Stakes

set to take this Group 2 contest before stepping back up to Group 1 company.

Tom Collins

STRADIVARIUS
Gold Cup

John Gosden's colt had a brilliant first season over staying trips in 2017, winning the Queen's Vase and Goodwood Cup along the way. He just failed in his hat-trick bid when third in the St Leger before filling the same berth behind Order Of St George on Champions Day at Ascot. His effortless victory on his reappearance in the Yorkshire Cup proved he has improved over the winter and he should be able to reverse the form with his old foe over this longer trip.

Paul Kealy

DESERT SKYLINE
Gold Cup

My original long-term fancy at a price was Rekindling but we haven't seen him yet and I can't see why Desert Skyline is 20-1 after his excellent second to Stradivarius at York. It's true the winner had a bit in hand there but Desert Skyline was conceding 3lb and the 1m6f trip would be an absolute minimum for him. He was very strong at the end when winning over 2m2f at Doncaster last year and could be in his element over 2m4f at Ascot.

Tom Park

CRYSTAL OCEAN
Hardwicke Stakes

Last season's St Leger was one of the hottest editions of the world's oldest Classic and the form has been franked numerous times already this season. Crystal Ocean was second that day to Capri and had the likes of Stradivarius, Coronet, Rekindling and Defoe behind him. He got back to winning ways at Sandown early this season before bolting up in a Group 3 at Newbury. The Hardwicke trip is perfect for this son of Sea The Stars and he looks

Nick Watts

EXPERT EYE
Commonwealth Cup

He could be interesting if he's dropped back in trip. A stab at the 2,000 Guineas didn't work out for him but he wasn't far off James Garfield at Newbury prior to that and sprint trips could be the making of him. He has problems settling and a strong pace over a shorter trip might help him fulfil his undoubted potential.

The star attraction

CRACKSMAN delivered the outstanding performance of last year's European Flat season in running away with the Champion Stakes at Ascot in October and, with even better expected of him this season, he will be a star attraction wherever he runs.

Even before being pointed towards Royal Ascot, he has lit up a grand occasion this year. He made his reappearance in late April at the reopening of Longchamp racecourse and produced a display in keeping with the stunning new look of Paris's premier racecourse.

Cracksman routed the opposition in the Group 1 Prix Ganay, powering clear to win by four lengths in an ideal start to his four-year-old season. "I can't be any more impressed, it was a great performance," jockey Frankie Dettori said afterwards.

The Ganay is the chief French stepping stone to the Prince of Wales's Stakes at Royal Ascot and victory continued Cracksman's winning run – all by wide margins – from the second half of last season. Three and a half lengths was the closest any rival finished to him as he romped through the Great Voltigeur Stakes at York, the Prix Niel at Chantilly and the Champion Stakes. That final success by an astonishing seven lengths earned him the title of European champion with an official rating of 130 – 2lb clear of stablemate Enable, the Prix de l'Arc de Triomphe winner – and demonstrated that Ascot's mile and a quarter brings out the best in him.

The one question mark about the Champion Stakes was that it was run on soft ground, which may have inconvenienced some of his rivals at the end of a long season. By the end of last year, Cracksman's only victory on good ground was his scrambled short-head win over Permian in the Derby Trial at Epsom.

The Ganay, then, was an important demonstration not just of his wellbeing after a winter of further growth and development, but of his ability to handle good ground at the top level. Trainer John Gosden believes he passed the test well, saying after the race: "The great thing is he's won today on good – it's slightly the faster side of good having walked it – so that's great, plus he goes in the soft."

The going was good to firm on all five days of Royal Ascot in 2017 and that would present a new test for Cracksman. It is probably one he will have to pass if he is to achieve all the ambitions held for him this summer.

STAR RATING
★★★★★

Owner: Anthony Oppenheimer
Trainer: John Gosden

AL SHAQAB

9
QIPCO

CRACKSMAN

'The Ganay was
an important
demonstration
not just of his
wellbeing but
of his ability to
handle good
ground at the
top level'

Tip Two Win

Owner: Mrs Anne Cowley
Trainer: Roger Teal

Real-life fairytale

MANY column inches during Royal Ascot will focus on blue-blooded breeding, both human and equine, but there is always room for a different kind of story. This year brings us Tip Two Win, described by owner-breeder Anne Cowley as her "fairytale horse".

Cowley's grey colt, trained by Roger Teal, was barely given a thought by most punters before being sent off at 50-1 for the Qipco 2,000 Guineas but there was no missing him in the race as he chased home Saxon Warrior, leaving better-fancied rivals from the more powerful training and breeding operations in his wake.

Tip Two Win's connections immediately looked towards the St James's Palace Stakes, the mile race for Guineas colts on the opening day of Royal Ascot, as another opportunity to take on the big guns at Group 1 level.

"We proved [in the Guineas] we're good enough to be in their company," Teal said. "It wasn't a fluke and I'm sure he'll back it up at Ascot. Hopefully we'll have a bit of fun that day as well."

Arriving at Royal Ascot would complete some journey for Tip Two Win, who started his racing career down the road at Windsor, with a win followed by a disappointing third last July, and spent his winter racing in Qatar. He won both starts there but those successes barely caused a ripple back home, hence his place among the outsiders in the Guineas.

He had been considered a high-class two-year-old by Teal, however, and finished second to the much-touted Elarqam (fourth in the Guineas) in the Group 3 Tattersalls Stakes at Newmarket last September.

He did not need to step up his level to win in Qatar but those wins around a right-hand bend will have prepared him for Ascot and another plus is the aplomb with which he handled the undulating track at Newmarket.

One thing is for sure: he will start much shorter in the betting at the royal meeting than the 50-1 he was sent off at Newmarket.

STAR RATING
★ ★ ★

Billesdon Brook

Owner: Pall Mall Partners
Trainer: Richard Hannon

Talented underdog

UNDERDOG winners aren't always greeted with wild acclaim in racing – after all, hardly anyone has backed them – but there was something a little different about Billesdon Brook's 66-1 victory in the Qipco 1,000 Guineas.

Not only did she make history as the longest-priced winner in the fillies' Classic, which dates back to 1814, but she did so for a group of owners who, while not exactly without a penny or two, had taken on and beaten racing's super rich with the Richard Hannon-trained longshot.

The 20-strong syndicate known as Pall Mall Partners – whose members include Richard Hannon snr – is headed by Jeanette McCreery, widow of Bob McCreery, who set up the group to race products of the family's Stowell Hill Stud in Somerset.

Having hit the jackpot with Classic success at Newmarket, the group can look to play up their winnings and a supplementary entry for the Coronation Stakes at a cost of £45,000 was immediately put on the agenda.

Her trainer is keen, having said her Guineas triumph was "a surprise but there was nothing fluky about it". Paul Curtis of Racing Post Ratings agreed, saying: "She travelled through the race like an improved filly and the form stacks up behind her."

Her RPR of 115 represented improvement of a stone from her previous best in a Group 3 win at Goodwood last August.

The task now is to do it again and the evidence from recent Guineas surprises is mixed. Seventeen horses have been placed in a Guineas at 33-1 or bigger in the past 20 years and eight of them never managed a win thereafter, while only two of the 12 who went on to Royal Ascot were successful there.

Those two were Zafeen, winner of the St James's Palace Stakes in 2003, and Ribchester, who won the Jersey Stakes in 2016 and then scored again at Royal Ascot last year in the Queen Anne Stakes.

The occasional gem can come out of a surprise result, then, but the odds will be stacked against Billesdon Brook at Royal Ascot once again. She couldn't overturn them again, could she?

STAR RATING
★★★

Gold Cup royalty

THERE might be high drama again when Order Of St George returns for another crack at the Gold Cup, which he won in 2016 before losing out by a short head last year in an epic battle with Big Orange.

This year offers the chance for Aidan O'Brien's star stayer to regain top billing in the biggest long-distance prize of the season and achieve a rare feat in the annals of Royal Ascot's oldest race.

If he succeeds this year, Order Of St George will be only the second horse after Kayf Tara (1998 and 2000) to regain the Gold Cup having lost in between – Anticipation won in 1816 and 1819 but without competing in the race in the intervening years.

There seems little doubt Order Of St George is up to the task. Not only is he a confirmed stayer, as he proved with his three-length success in the 2016 Gold Cup, he is also a class act over middle distances, having finished third and fourth in the last two runnings of the Prix de l'Arc de Triomphe.

Last year's Arc run behind Enable was his only defeat in four runs after Royal Ascot and he showed his quality by beating subsequent Melbourne Cup winner Rekindling in a Group 3 at the Curragh and old rival Torcedor on two occasions – by nine lengths in the Irish St Leger and then by a much closer margin, just half a length, in the British Champions Long Distance Cup back at Ascot in October.

That level of form makes him a cut above his rival stayers and he was rated 123 in the 2017 Longines World's Best Racehorse Rankings – the highest figure over extended distances (beyond 1m5½f), with a trio rated 3lb behind him. Not only did that make Order Of St George the world's top stayer, he was joint 12th in the overall standings alongside the likes of Highland Reel, his stablemate who won the Prince of Wales's Stakes at Royal Ascot last year.

An area of concern is that Order Of St George has been beaten four times at odds-on, including three of the last five occasions when he has been that short at Group 1 or 2 level. But he clearly ran to a high standard in last year's Gold Cup and his defeat arguably stemmed from being left with too much to do by Ryan Moore – a rare slip that is unlikely to be repeated.

As Moore said after Order Of St George's reappearance victory at Navan in April, "he's the best horse in the division." Many punters will be banking on him to prove it in this year's Gold Cup.

STAR RATING
★ ★ ★ ★

Owner: M Tabor, D Smith, Mrs Magnier, LJ Williams
Trainer: Aidan O'Brien

'Not only is he a confirmed
stayer, he is also a class act
over middle distances'

Serious contender

'He's a very
talented horse
who has
not stopped
improving'

BENBATL is a Royal Ascot winner already, having landed last year's Group 3 Hampton Court Stakes, and now his mission is to do it again at the top level in the Queen Anne Stakes or the Prince of Wales's Stakes.

The Godolphin colt came up short in his attempts in Group 1 company as a three-year-old last season, finishing fifth to Wings Of Eagles in that frantic finish to the Derby at Epsom and in the same position behind the top-class Enable in the King George VI and Queen Elizabeth Stakes at Ascot in July.

Enable left him trailing by 11 and a half lengths and runner-up Ulysses was seven lengths ahead, which left Benbatl with considerable ground to make up in order to become competitive at the top level. He made great strides in four runs at Meydan over the winter, however, and returned to British shores as a Group 1 winner and with a Racing Post Rating of 123, 8lb better than he ended last season.

The Group 1 victory came on his final start at Meydan on World Cup night when he produced a dominant performance to take the 1m1f Dubai Turf by three and a half lengths. Runner-up Vivlos had landed the same race 12 months earlier – when subsequent Queen

Anne winner Ribchester was third – and Real Steel, fourth behind Benbatl, had won the Dubai Turf in 2016.

Trainer Saeed Bin Suroor believes Benbatl is unlucky not to be a dual Group 1 winner, having been forced to race wide when beaten less than a length into second in the Jebel Hatta three weeks before World Cup night, and there is no doubt he has a serious prospect on his hands.

Bin Suroor has not had a Group 1 winner at Royal Ascot since Colour Vision took the Gold Cup six years ago but, if Benbatl's improvement is genuine and can be taken further, this is just the type of blossoming older horse with whom he excelled for many years.

The intermediate distance of 1m1f for Benbatl's Group 1 assignments at Meydan gives Bin Suroor plenty of options and he is confident for the season ahead. "He's a very talented horse who has not stopped improving and he showed a fantastic turn of foot when winning the Dubai Turf. We're looking to campaign him in all the top races between a mile and 1m2f," he says.

Good or fast ground will suit Benbatl – it was good to firm when he won at Royal Ascot last year – and he is one to take seriously.

STAR RATING

★ ★ ★ ★

Haunted by hoodoo

FOUR runs at Ascot, four defeats. It's not the most promising form line for one of the big favourites heading towards this year's royal meeting but that's the trouble with Harry – he's no angel when it comes to Ascot.

While the Clive Cox-trained speedster has met defeat there on four occasions, his record is perfect everywhere else with five wins from his appearances at Newbury, Haydock (twice), Newmarket and York. It is quite a conundrum, and one that will have to be rectified double-quick if the champion sprinter is to stop his crown slipping on this royal occasion.

All of the Ascot defeats could be excused, to varying degrees. The first was on his debut as a two-year-old in May 2016 and he lost by just a nose, a promising enough start. Almost exactly a year later he made his first appearance as a three-year-old there as well and ran an encouraging second to the smart Blue Point, his Godolphin ownermate, before reversing the form when they met again six

weeks later in the Commonwealth Cup at the royal meeting.

The problem was that Harry Angel was forced to settle for second place again as Caravaggio zoomed past him and Blue Point to score by three-quarters of a length. At that stage Caravaggio looked in pole position for champion sprinter honours but then Harry Angel beat him in the July Cup and defeated Blue Point again in the Haydock Sprint Cup – along with the likes of Tasleet and The Tin Man on both occasions – to stake a much stronger claim to the crown.

In the end Harry Angel shared the title with five-furlong flyer Battaash, even though his season ended on a low with fourth place behind Librisa Breeze in the British Champions Sprint at Ascot in October. This time the excuse was that the run came at the end of a long, hard season, but it was still another Ascot defeat to blot his copybook.

This season opened with a smooth success in the Duke of York Stakes – a key stepping stone to the Diamond

Jubilee Stakes – and encouragingly it was the first time Harry Angel had won on his initial appearance of the year.

Cox is not worried about the Ascot record – "people mention he's never won there but I don't think there's anything to read into that" – and is looking forward to another exciting assault on the top sprints. "He's a once-in-a-lifetime horse. He makes the heart race every occasion you see him on the racetrack," the trainer says.

On Racing Post Ratings none of Harry Angel's likely rivals can touch him. He hit a high of 128 last year – as did Battaash – but next best were Caravaggio and Lady Aurelia, the King's Stand Stakes winner, on 124. This Angel has wings. He just needs to prove he can fly at Ascot.

STAR RATING
★ ★ ★ ★ ★

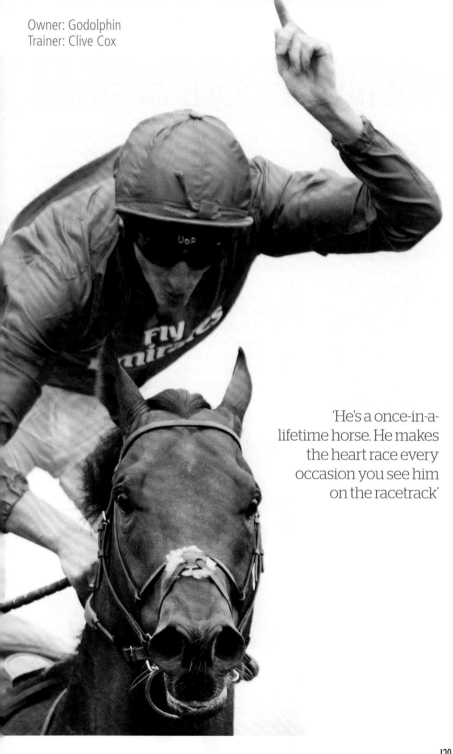

'He's a once-in-a-lifetime horse. He makes the heart race every occasion you see him on the racetrack'

Clemmie

Owner: Michael Tabor, Derrick Smith & Sue Magnier
Trainer: Aidan O'Brien

Family honour at stake

SOME family score-settling might be in order if Clemmie makes a return trip to Royal Ascot this year.

Her year-older brother Churchill was victorious at the 2016 royal meeting, in the Chesham Stakes as a juvenile, but last year he finished a hugely disappointing fourth at odds of 1-2 in the St James's Palace Stakes. Three days later Clemmie added to the family woes when she was beaten almost five lengths into seventh place in the Group 3 Albany Stakes behind French raider Different League.

From there the siblings took different paths. Churchill – named after the first of the 13 prime ministers who have served during the Queen's reign – was retired to stud at the end of last season after a career that brought four Group 1 victories including the 2,000 Guineas and Irish 2,000 Guineas but no more success once his seven-race winning streak had been brought to an end in the St James's Palace.

Meanwhile, after a slow start that saw her defeated in a 6f Curragh maiden as well as the Albany, Clemmie – named after Churchill's wife

– quickly blossomed into a high-class performer last summer.

Nine days after her Royal Ascot run, she won a Group 3 at the Curragh and 12 days after that she stepped up another level to land the Group 2 Duchess of Cambridge Stakes at the Newmarket July meeting. Finally, after a good rest, she rounded off her juvenile season with Group 1 success in the Cheveley Park Stakes on Newmarket's other track.

One measure of Clemmie's improvement over the

summer was that Different League, her Albany conqueror, finished a length and three-quarters behind in second in the Cheveley Park, and another was that she had gone from a Racing Post Rating of 92 at Royal Ascot to 114 on her final run.

Her progress was interrupted this spring when a hold-up in her preparation forced her to miss the 1,000 Guineas at Newmarket. That would have been an opportunity to join her brother on one roll of honour but Royal Ascot offers another, as well as the chance to right some wrongs.

STAR RATING
★★★★

Teppal

Owner: Sheikh Mohammed Bin Khalifa Al Thani
Trainer: David Simcock

Classic prizefighter

TEPPAL made the giant leap from novice winner on the Kempton all-weather as a juvenile to Classic heroine on her reappearance in May when she landed a dramatic running of the Poule d'Essai des Pouliches (French 1,000 Guineas) at Longchamp.

In a frenetic finish, Teppal (*below, 2*) came with a strong late run to snatch the lead and hold on by a short neck from Coeur De Beaute with Wind Chimes just a head behind in third and the same distance back to fourth-placed Capla Temptress. It was messy, it was scrappy, but none of that mattered to Newmarket trainer David Simcock as he celebrated his first Classic success.

It was testament to Simcock's skill that he had Teppal ready for a Group 1 first time out after just two runs as a juvenile. She won both of those 7f races, first at Lingfield on turf before switching to the all-weather, and showed a fair deal of promise without looking obvious Classic material.

Part of the doubt stemmed from her pedigree, which suggested she might not handle the step up to a mile, but her strong finish at Longchamp laid that to rest.

Even so, the Pouliches looked below its usual strength this year – Capla Temptress was the only one of the first six who had run in a Group 1 – and that was reflected in a Racing Post Rating of 107 for Teppal.

That represented a big step up from her juvenile mark of 90 but still put her behind the first five from the 1,000 Guineas at Newmarket, where surprise winner Billesdon Brook earned an RPR of 115.

The Royal Ascot battleground for Guineas fillies is the Coronation Stakes and that contest was the immediate thought in Simcock's mind after the Pouliches.

Teppal may have more to find on the form book but she deserves to take her chance in an open-looking year. If it comes to a battle royal, this is one filly who will not shirk from the fight.

STAR RATING
★★★

Sheema Classic ace is

THIS time last year Godolphin had high hopes for impressive Dubai Sheema Classic winner Jack Hobbs but he turned out to be one of the flops of Royal Ascot when he trailed home last of eight behind Highland Reel in the Prince of Wales's Stakes.

Having won the Sheema Classic in dominant style again this year with Hawkbill, Godolphin will be hoping he can fly the flag with considerably more gusto at the 2018 royal meeting. There is less hype around the Charlie Appleby-trained five-year-old than there was with Jack Hobbs but the signs in Dubai pointed to the prospect of a solid campaign.

"He's now becoming what we'd call the good old-fashioned Godolphin horse who can be campaigned abroad," Appleby said just

'He's been flagged up as a soft-ground specialist but he only just got beat in a Grade 1 in Canada on very quick ground'

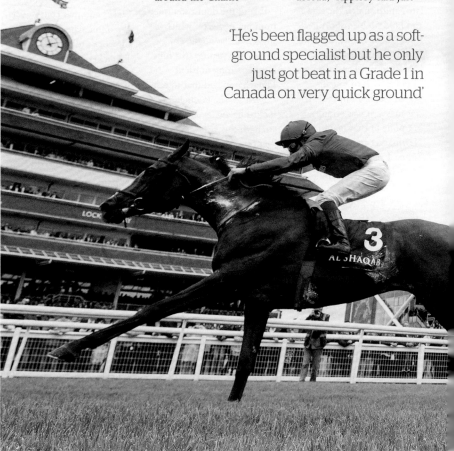

solid Group 1 material

before the Sheema Classic win.

Whereas Jack Hobbs appeared to be still on the way up 12 months ago before he crashed and burned, Hawkbill is on something of a comeback. Two years ago he was a Royal Ascot winner in the Group 3 Hampton Court Stakes and quickly followed up with Group 1 success in the Eclipse at Sandown, but thereafter he struggled to reach the same heights.

From the Eclipse up to the end of last season, he won only twice in ten starts – at Group 2 and Group 3 level – and was regularly well beaten in Group 1 company. There were some

better signs in the second half of last season, however, and he stepped up again during his winter campaign in Dubai.

Now aged five, he won a Group 2 at Meydan on Super Saturday in early March and then struck for the first time at Group 1 level since the Eclipse when he surged three lengths clear of Poet's Word and Arc runner-up Cloth Of Stars in the Sheema Classic.

That performance merited a Racing Post Rating of 119, still 2lb below his Eclipse best but nevertheless a return to Group 1 standard.

The form book suggests he prefers cut in the ground – in 2016 he struck a

soft-ground year when he won the Hampton Court Stakes and then the Eclipse – but Appleby argues against that view. "He's been flagged up as a soft-ground specialist but he only just got beat in a Grade 1 in Canada on very quick ground," he says.

As a Group 1 winner at 1m2½f and 1m4f, Hawkbill has a versatility that is so useful in an older horse and the options at the royal meeting are the Prince of Wales's Stakes and the Hardwicke Stakes. If fast ground is not an issue, he looks set to be a solid challenger.

STAR RATING

★ ★ ★

Up for the challenge

THE Prix de l'Arc de Triomphe could be the ultimate aim with Defoe this season, which tells you plenty about how highly trainer Roger Varian rates the up-and-coming four-year-old.

Further indication comes from the fact that Defoe is entered in the Group 1 Prince of Wales's Stakes as well as the Group 2 Hardwicke Stakes at Royal Ascot, but you don't have to read between the entry lines to work out Varian's thinking because he has told us directly.

"We love this horse," Varian said in his Stable Tour in the Racing Post in April. "He flopped in the Leger but he wasn't quite right when we got him home. It's an old cliche but it was too bad a run to be true. He was very progressive before that and his Geoffrey Freer win at Newbury was eyecatchingly good. He's by Dalakhani out of a Pivotal mare, so there's every reason to think he'll be better at four. He hasn't got masses of miles on the clock – he's got a good race in him."

Soon after that Stable Tour visit, Defoe set about proving Varian right. Within the week the grey colt had won the Group 3 John Porter Stakes at Newbury – a well-established staging post for older middle-distance horses on the way to Royal

'It's hard to disagree with Varian's opinion that there is a good race in him'

Ascot – and he quickly added the Group 2 Jockey Club Stakes at Newmarket.

In powering clear on both occasions, Defoe demonstrated he was ready for better-class company. At Newbury he scored by two and a half lengths from Danehill Kodiac, a good yardstick who then finished runner-up to Idaho – last year's Hardwicke winner – by three and a half lengths in the Group 3 Ormonde Stakes at Chester. After that the Newmarket race hardly tested Defoe as he scored by three and three-quarter lengths from Red Verdon.

Those victories resumed the upwardly mobile profile of Defoe's three-year-old season when he carried a winning run from handicaps to Listed level and the Group 3 Geoffrey Freer Stakes at Newbury before the progress was interrupted abruptly when he trailed home tenth behind Capri in the St Leger, having been well fancied.

The St Leger was Defoe's first foray into Group 1 company but it has to be written off as a non-event for him. It's hard to disagree with Varian's opinion that there is a good race in him and it wouldn't be a great surprise if it was one as good as those up for grabs at Royal Ascot.

STAR RATING
★ ★ ★

135

Gustav Klimt

Owner: Sue Magnier, Michael Tabor & Derrick Smith
Trainer: Aidan O'Brien

More battles lie ahead

PLENTY of early Classic hopefuls are forced to drop to a lower level, or into obscurity, after those hopes have been dashed but judging Gustav Klimt on his sixth place in the Qipco 2,000 Guineas might be too harsh.

There is a strong argument for saying Royal Ascot is the true early marker for how the season will pan out among the top three-year-olds and that we should wait and see how the picture looks for the milers after the St James's Palace Stakes – and nowadays for the young sprinters after the Commonwealth Cup.

Saxon Warrior was the strongest of Aidan O'Brien's challengers in the 2,000 Guineas market on the day and much the most powerful in the race as he claimed a decisive victory, with stablemate Gustav Klimt almost four lengths adrift.

But Gustav Klimt would not be the first to get up off the floor after Guineas defeat at Newmarket and come back punching at Royal Ascot. Since 2000 eight beaten Guineas horses have won the St James's Palace the following month and a pertinent example might be the O'Brien-trained Mastercraftsman, who was beaten just over four lengths into fifth at Newmarket in 2009 before winning at Royal Ascot.

Of O'Brien's seven St James's Palace winners, Mastercraftsman is one of four who were beaten on their first Group 1 assignment of the season in a Guineas.

Many of O'Brien's Classic contenders are tested in Group 1 company as two-year-olds to prepare them for the battles ahead, but that was not the case with Gustav Klimt. His juvenile campaign was cut short when he suffered a setback after winning the Group 2 Superlative Stakes at the Newmarket July meeting and O'Brien made sure he brought him back early this season to gain some extra conditioning, with the fourth race of Gustav Klimt's short career bringing victory in the 2,000 Guineas Trial at Leopardstown after an absence of 273 days.

There was plenty to like about that winning comeback. Keeping on under hands and heels riding by Ryan Moore, Gustav Klimt got up late on to beat Imaging, who won at Listed level on his next start. This Klimt remains a work in progress.

STAR RATING
★★★★

Poet's Word

Owner: Saeed Suhail
Trainer: Sir Michael Stoute

Rapid rise to high level

POET'S WORD was something of a nearly horse last year. Having nearly won the Huxley Stakes at Chester in May, he nearly went to Royal Ascot for the Hardwicke Stakes but didn't. Then in the autumn he nearly won the Group 1 Irish Champion Stakes, beaten half a length by Decorated Knight.

Even so, that represented considerable progress for this Sir Michael Stoute-trained late developer considering he had started his season in April by winning a Chelmsford handicap and just five months later had made it to Group 1 company, via Group 3 victory at Goodwood in August.

He confirmed he belonged at the top level with another second place in the Champion Stakes at Ascot in October – this time beaten seven lengths by Cracksman, but with Highland Reel a neck behind him – and yet another in the Dubai Sheema Classic in March, three lengths adrift of Hawkbill but again in front of plenty of good horses.

Now aged five, and with top-level form at 1m2f and 1m4f, he is entered for the Group 1 Prince of Wales's Stakes and the Group 2 Hardwicke at Royal Ascot, although Cracksman may well bar his way again in the top-level event.

Stoute had enough belief in Poet's Word to want to go for the Group 1 Eclipse over 1m2f early last summer, which is instructive in itself, although owner Saeed Suhail believed at the time it would be better to stick to 1m4f.

Both routes remain open, although a deciding factor may well be whether the ground has the bit of juice he seems to prefer. With a Racing Post Rating of 120 for his Irish Champion run and still room for improvement, Poet's Word is one to watch.

STAR RATING
★★★

Quick fix could work

IF YOU had carried out a straw poll on where US Navy Flag was most likely to end up at Royal Ascot after he had finished fifth in the French 2,000 Guineas, the majority might well have come out in favour of the Commonwealth Cup.

That Group 1 sprint, first run in 2015, is a quick fix nowadays for any three-year-old who falls short over the Classic mile and there would not be great surprise if trainer Aidan O'Brien took that option with US Navy Flag.

Many thought US Navy Flag looked more of a sprint type after a busy two-year-old campaign that featured Group 1 wins in the Middle Park and Dewhurst Stakes among ten runs in a six-month period from the beginning of May. He stretched out to 7f to land the Dewhurst but was left well behind in tenth over 1m½f on his final start of last season in the Breeders' Cup Juvenile. Possibly that defeat was down to the distance, the fast pace, the dirt surface or the effect of a hard season – or any combination of those factors –

but even then sprinting looked a likely option.

The defeats continued into the new campaign for last season's European champion two-year-old but he can't be judged too harshly for his opening two losses. After finishing last of the four runners on unsuitably heavy ground in the 2,000 Guineas Trial won by stablemate Gustav Klimt at Leopardstown in April, Longchamp was the next port of call for the French Guineas but again the

ground wouldn't have been quite fast enough to bring out the best in US Navy Flag.

He raced from stall 11 and stumbled rounding the turn for home before finishing a creditable fifth in the circumstances. O'Brien had already made the point that US Navy Flag did not win until his fifth start as a juvenile – on the fourth he was only 14th in last year's Coventry Stakes at the royal meeting – and might take time to hit his peak again.

Dropping back in trip to tackle the Commonwealth Cup, a race Ballydoyle won 12 months ago with Caravaggio, is a real proposition and there's no reason why he couldn't develop into a top-notch sprinter if he goes down that road.

There is a precedent, of course. Three years ago Muhaarar was eighth in the French Guineas before dropping to 6f to land the inaugural Commonwealth Cup, the first in a run of four Group 1 wins that carried him to the champion sprinter title.

STAR RATING
★★★★

Owner: Derrick Smith,
Sue Magnier & Michael Tabor
Trainer: Aidan O'Brien

'There's no reason why he couldn't develop into a top-notch sprinter if he goes down that road'

France's star stayer

BRITISH and Irish racegoers have long been denied a glimpse of the staying king across the water, as a combination of first caution and then injury have prevented Vazirabad from travelling to Ascot or Goodwood up until now.

Even from afar the six-year-old son of Manduro exudes star quality and has a glittering record to match, having won three French Group 1s – a pair of Prix Royal-Oak titles and a middling-standard renewal of the Prix du Cadran in 2017 – as well as a hat-trick of Dubai Gold Cups.

Those triumphs at Meydan show that neither a trip away from his native Chantilly nor potentially fast ground can be held up as a negative for Vazirabad, while his performances in the Cadran (he was a narrow second to Quest For More in 2016) prove that the 2m4f of the Gold Cup is within his compass.

Vazirabad's greatest strength is also the point of most concern for his trainer, Alain de Royer-Dupre. He has a high cruising speed and an exceptional turn of foot for a stayer, but his acceleration tends to come in a relatively short burst and Christophe Soumillon has

had to learn to wait as late as possible before delivering his challenge.

From that point of view, connections will want to avoid Vazirabad joining issue with the likes of Order Of St George and Stradivarius for as long as possible in a race that can often turn into a war of attrition up the straight.

It would be unfair on Vazirabad to say he got outbattled by Ice Breeze in last season's Royal-Oak, however, as his younger challenger had a not insignificant weight-for-age pull and would be an interesting contender himself for the Gold Cup if owner Khalid Abdullah and trainer Pascal Bary decided to take up the challenge.

Vazirabad's chief market rivals at Royal Ascot showed Group 1 form over middle distances earlier in their careers but he does not look outclassed. While he has tended to excel at or around 2m, he cut through his rivals in eyecatching style off blistering fractions in the Dubai Gold Cup in March and was regarded highly enough to be tried in the 1m4f Grand Prix de Saint-Cloud as a four-year-old.

The current Aga Khan tasted Gold Cup success 19

years ago thanks to the John Oxx-trained Enzeli and Vazirabad would be a worthy addition to the race's roll of honour.

STAR RATING
★ ★ ★ ★

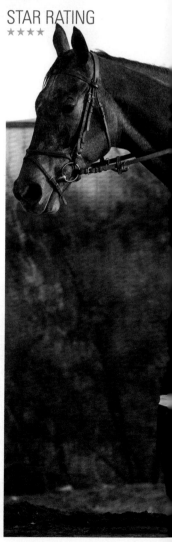

Owner: H H Aga Khan
Trainer: Alain de Royer-Dupre

'He has a high cruising speed and an
exceptional turn of foot for a stayer,
but his acceleration tends to come
in a relatively short burst'

Chance to shine

COMPETING with a popular and talented older brother can be difficult, as Idaho found out last year when he finished sixth to Highland Reel in the Group 1 Coronation Cup at Epsom.

A few weeks later the two brothers shared the stage successfully at Royal Ascot, albeit with Highland Reel in a starring role in the Group 1 Prince of Wales's Stakes and Idaho among the supporting cast with his Group 2 Hardwicke Stakes victory.

When, finally, Idaho did get his head in front of Highland Reel, hardly anyone took any notice because they were both well beaten in third and fourth behind wonder filly Enable in the King George VI and Queen Elizabeth Stakes.

Now, at the age of five, Idaho has the stage to himself and it could be his season to shine. Highland Reel is a hard act to follow, having gone to stud with seven Group 1 wins and the prize-money record for a European-trained horse, but at least Idaho is no longer in direct competition with his year-older brother.

The obvious route back to Royal Ascot for trainer Aidan

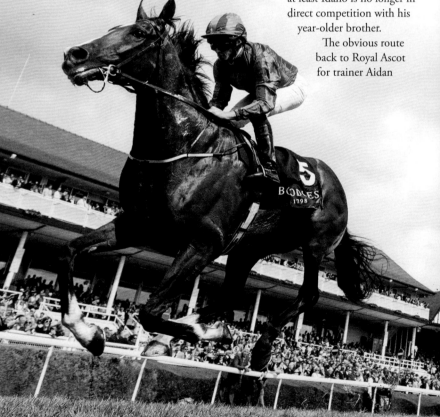

O'Brien is an attempt at a Hardwicke double, last achieved by Maraahel in 2006-07, but fresh possibilities opened up after Idaho's victory in the Ormonde Stakes at Chester in May. That win over 1m5½f was a step up in trip from his usual 1m4f and he did it strongly under Ryan Moore, scoring by three and a half lengths from useful yardstick Danehill Kodiac

to bring the Gold Cup at Ascot into play. There is also the tempter of the Weatherbys Hamilton Stayers' Million – the £1m prize if a horse wins one of the four staying prep races in May (of which the Ormonde was one) and goes on to take the Gold Cup, the Goodwood Cup in July and the Lonsdale Cup at York in August.

"Ryan was very happy with how well he stayed and we could look at another plan if needed. It leaves us with more options," O'Brien said.

"He's maturing well and starting to do things right. He's travelled the world and

is getting very professional now. It was good to see him pull clear the way he did and Ryan said he didn't think he would have any problems going further."

Having ended last season with a Racing Post Rating of 122, earned with his King George third, Idaho is not far off the 124 peak of Highland Reel, but what he has yet to show is the hardiness and winning spirit to produce at a high level time after time.

Maybe this season it will come. He certainly has the pedigree for it.

STAR RATING
★★★

'He's maturing well and starting to do things right. He's travelled the world and is getting very professional'

Owner: Sheikh Hamdan Bin Mohammed Al Maktoum
Trainer: Mark Johnston

Trainer on familiar path

A PIECE of sound advice at Royal Ascot for many years has been to watch out for a strong-staying, improving three-year-old trained by Mark Johnston. And the one to watch this year may well be Mildenberger.

Immediately after a major Derby trial like the Dante Stakes, most heads turn towards Epsom but Mildenberger *(below left)* was not entered for the Derby and Johnston was already mulling over Royal Ascot options with the Dante runner-up. "We've got him and Dee Ex Bee for the same owner and we've got the Derby, King Edward VII

Stakes and Queen's Vase to think about. Long term, we have the St Leger in our sights. The King Edward VII and Queen's Vase are a big lure."

Mildenberger was well put in his place in the Dante by Roaring Lion, who scored by four and a half lengths, but that should not preclude a good run at Ascot. Johnston is convinced the 1m2½f at York was too short – "there's no doubt he wants further, how much further only time will tell" – and in the past decade three beaten horses from the Dante have gone on to win at the royal meeting, as well as Johnston's

Permian, who won the Dante and then the King Edward VII last year having been tenth in the Derby in between.

Permian was a third winner of the King Edward VII for Johnston, who counts the Queen's Vase as his most successful race at the meeting with seven victories. In the past decade he has had five winners from 21 runners in those two contests at a strike-rate of 24 per cent. That makes Mildenberger one to take seriously.

STAR RATING
★★★

Coeur De Beaute

Owner: Teruya Yoshida
Trainer: Mauricio Delcher Sanchez

Better luck next time

A CASE could be made for any of the principals from the Poule d'Essai des Pouliches (French 1,000 Guineas) coming out on top in a rematch, such was the tightness of the finish, and Coeur De Beaute's connections would have one of the strongest arguments.

If trainer Mauricio Delcher Sanchez and new owner Teruya Yoshida decide to send her to Royal Ascot for the Coronation Stakes – the traditional showdown of Guineas fillies from around Europe – Coeur De Beaute *(yellow stars)* could prove capable of stepping up to the challenge.

Sanchez's filly finished fast in the Pouliches but was beaten a short neck by British raider Teppal, with the Andre Fabre-trained Wind Chimes a head behind in third and Marco Botti's Capla Temptress another head back in fourth.

A significant factor in the result may have been that the race was switched at late notice to Longchamp's outer track – renowned for disadvantaging those drawn wide – and the fast finishers Coeur De Beaute and Wind Chimes came from the two outside stalls. Teppal, who was drawn near the inside,

did not have the clearest run herself, leaving plenty of room for post-race argument.

What is hard to dispute is Coeur De Beaute's improvement this year. The best of her six runs as a juvenile was a Listed success over 6f at Maisons-Laffitte on very soft going in October but she improved on her reappearance to win the Group 3 Prix Imprudence over 7f at Deauville, this time on heavy ground.

The Pouliches marked another step forward in Group 1 company over a mile and the good ground

did not hinder her. More will be needed in the Coronation, and faster going might be an issue, but her strong finish at Longchamp suggested she has not reached her limit.

Sanchez certainly should not be underestimated if he decides to run Coeur De Beaute. His name is on the Royal Ascot roll of honour already with Equiano, who took the 2008 King's Stand Stakes at 22-1 before winning the race again two years later after being transferred to Barry Hills.

STAR RATING

★★★

145

One for Cup shortlist

THE Pavilion Stakes, a Group 3 at Ascot that takes place about seven weeks before the big meeting, is one of those races that could easily pass you by. But the result has been well worth noting in the past three years, with Limato, Harry Angel and Blue Point all making their mark en route to big runs at Royal Ascot and beyond.

The reason is simple: since the Group 1 Commonwealth Cup was introduced at Royal Ascot in 2015, the Pavilion – likewise for three-year-olds over six furlongs – has become a key trial for the big race. And for that simple reason Invincible Army, this year's clear-cut winner of the Pavilion, has to be on the Commonwealth Cup shortlist.

Invincible Army was a first Group winner for his up-and-coming trainer James Tate when he won last year's Group 3 Sirenia Stakes in a juvenile course record at Kempton and, having doubled that tally in the Pavilion by stretching a length and a half clear under Ryan Moore, the speedy son of Invincible Spirit raised hopes that he can go much further.

"Ryan loved him and thought he was a really nice horse. He said the ground was as soft as he would want it and that he's definitely a proper Group horse," Tate said.

"We knew he had trained on, it's just a question of how far we can go."

Judging by the recent history of the Pavilion, that might be pretty far. Limato won in 2015 before finishing second to champion sprinter Muhaarar in the first running of the Commonwealth Cup and later adding Group 1 wins in the July Cup and Prix de la Foret, while last year's one-two Blue Point and Harry Angel filled the places behind Caravaggio in the Commonwealth Cup. Harry Angel then became a July Cup winner, like Limato, and ended last season as joint champion sprinter.

Invincible Army still has a lot to prove but at the same time Tate cannot be sure of exactly what he has on his hands, saying: "Nothing can go with him at home, he just sweeps everything aside."

Summer conditions at the royal meeting would not worry Tate – "I don't see him as a soft-ground horse, I see him as a good horse who wants good ground," he says – and he is also confident Invincible Army has the pace

to live at the highest level. "There's half a chance after Royal Ascot he could try five [furlongs] one day, as I think he's pretty fast."

STAR RATING
★ ★ ★

'Nothing can go with him at home, he just sweeps everything aside'

As tough as they come

FIGHTING back against the odds to rescue a career and score at the top level is the sort of heartwarming story more readily associated with one of the smaller racing stables, not Aidan O'Brien's all-conquering Ballydoyle operation.

Yet that is precisely what Rhododendron has achieved

under O'Brien's careful handling and, having landed the Group 1 Lockinge Stakes in May, she is in prime position for one of Royal Ascot's biggest prizes less than a year after a harrowing experience in the French Oaks.

Recalling that traumatic day at Chantilly, O'Brien said after the Lockinge: "She bled the worst I have ever seen. She exploded in the race and all the horses and jockeys were covered in her blood. I think maybe it was the heat that day – it was 30C at Chantilly. We were very worried for her – it is very rare for a horse to come back from something like that."

Rhododendron *(below right)*, remarkably, has come back just as good as before – and possibly better. Above all, her fighting spirit is intact, as she showed with her hard-earned short-head victory over Lightning Spear in the Lockinge. For several moments inside the final furlong, it seemed as if she would have to settle for second best but she kept responding gamely to Ryan Moore's urging to force the victory at the line.

Last autumn, back at Chantilly less than four months after the French Oaks ordeal, she had battled to another narrow victory over stablemate Hydrangea in the Group 1 Prix de l'Opera and then had gone down by just a length to Wuheida in the Breeders' Cup Filly & Mare Turf at Del Mar.

She was a Group 1 winner

at two in the Fillies' Mile, again over Hydrangea, at three over 1m2f and now back at a mile again as a four-year-old, which gives O'Brien the option of keeping her at the shorter trip for the Queen Anne Stakes – the usual destination for Lockinge winners – or going back up to 1m2f for the Prince of Wales's Stakes.

O'Brien once seemed to regard 1m2f as the optimum trip for Rhododendron but clearly she is well suited by a hard-run mile on fast ground, which is what she had in the Lockinge.

Most ominously for her rivals, O'Brien revealed after the Lockinge: "She is going to improve again – she hasn't been on the grass gallop yet."

STAR RATING

★★★★

'She is going to improve again – she hasn't been on the grass gallop yet'

Life in the fast lane

LEAVE them wanting more. That was certainly what Battaash achieved on his final appearance of last season when he sped to an exhilarating four-length victory in the Group 1 Prix de l'Abbaye at Chantilly. There are few better sights in Flat racing than a top-notch sprinter in full flow and the thought of seeing Battaash back in Group 1 action is one of the most exciting elements of the 2018 season.

First stop on his Group 1 schedule should be the King's Stand Stakes and a potential showdown with last year's winner, the US speedball Lady Aurelia. What a mouthwatering prospect that is.

Lady A won the 2017 King's Stand by three lengths in similarly dominant fashion to Battaash's Abbaye, whch was done and dusted by halfway, and they are lined up for a speed duel of the highest order.

Trainer Charlie Hills was in awe of Battaash last year as he made rapid progress from a Racing Post Rating of 101 as a juvenile to 128 by the end of his three-year-old campaign, which took

him through Listed, Group 3, Group 2 and finally Group 1 success.

"I've never seen anything so fast on the gallops in my life," Hills said. "When he goes past, you just think 'oh my lord'. It's like two horses against one when he works – he can go past at double the speed of anything else."

There is another side to Battaash, however, and it is one that may come into

> I've never seen anything so fast on the gallops in my life. It's like two horses against one when he works – he can go past at double the speed of anything else'

play amid the hubbub of Royal Ascot.

"He's got a bit of a short fuse and when he loses it, he loses it properly," admitted Hills, who saw Battaash lose his first chance of Group 1 glory at York last summer after boiling over before

the Nunthorpe Stakes.

Fourth place in the Nunthorpe was Battaash's only defeat in five starts during a dazzling campaign that earned him the title of Europe's joint champion sprinter alongside Harry Angel.

Since 2000 their RPR of 128 has been bettered by only three other European-trained sprinters – Mozart (2001), Oasis Dream (2003) and Dream Ahead (2011) all had an RPR of 129.

No wonder there is such anticipation at seeing Battaash in top-level action again as he goes for his first Group 1 win on home soil, especially with Hills having reported that he grew an inch and a half and put on 30kg over the winter.

A bigger, more powerful Battaash? That's a scary thought for those trying to take him on but it's exciting for Royal Ascot racegoers.

"I'd love him to be the kind of horse that people follow, the way they follow Winx," said Hills. With his heady brew of talent and temperament, Battaash might just be that kind of horse.

STAR RATING
★★★★★

Going for gold

THE Gold Cup, with its historical prestige and winner's purse of almost £285,000, is one of the prime targets of the Flat season but for Torcedor's connections there are a million other reasons to go for it this year.

The Irish stayer is one of those eligible for the new Weatherbys Hamilton Stayers' Million, which offers a prize of £1 million for a horse winning one of four recognised prep races in May – the Sagaro Stakes at Ascot, the Ormonde Stakes at Chester, the Yorkshire Cup or the Henry II Stakes at Sandown – and going on to take the Gold Cup, the Goodwood Cup in July and the Lonsdale Cup at York in August.

The £1 million would be split between the connections of the successful horse, with 70 per cent awarded to the owner and 30 per cent divided equally between the trainer, stable staff, breeder and jockey.

Torcedor was the first to stake a claim when he won the earliest of the preps, the Sagaro, by an impressive five lengths. The Jessica Harrington-trained six-year-old took the race by the scruff of the neck and coasted to a front-running victory, just four weeks after trailing home last behind star French stayer Vazirabad over 2m at Meydan on Dubai World Cup night.

Harrington put a line through the Meydan run – "I'd say it was the travelling, it might have been a bridge too far" – and is focused on Ascot and the bonus.

The problem is that old rival Order Of St George, the 2016 Gold Cup winner and last year's narrow runner-up, stands in the way, which helps to explain

'He is from the family of four-time Gold Cup winner Yeats and we may not have seen the best of him at marathon trips'

why one bookmaker quoted Torcedor at 100-1 to land the bonus.

Torcedor caused an upset in their first meeting early last season, scoring by a length and a half in the Group 3 Vintage Crop Stakes at Navan, but then finished fifth in the Gold Cup and runner-up to Order Of St George in the Group 1 Irish St Leger and the Group 2 Long Distance Cup at Ascot.

The margin was a yawning nine lengths in the Irish St Leger but Torcedor cut it to half a length at Ascot, being caught close home after taking a clear lead early in the straight.

That race was 2m, which raises doubt about whether Torcedor can stay the extra half-mile of the Gold Cup even with hold-up tactics, although the counter-argument is that he is from the family of four-time Gold Cup winner Yeats and we may not have seen the best of him at marathon trips.

STAR RATING
★ ★ ★

So near and yet so far

NEWMARKET trainer David Simcock enjoyed a tremendous spring, topped by a first Classic success with Teppal in the French 1,000 Guineas, and he went agonisingly close to another big-race victory when Lightning Spear was just touched off by Rhododendron in the Lockinge Stakes.

That short-head defeat was the latest chapter in a long story of near-misses for Lightning Spear, who is now in his fourth season of competing in Group 1 company but has yet to win at that level. The seven-year-old has been placed in five Group 1 contests, including the Queen Anne Stakes at Royal Ascot and twice in the Lockinge.

He looks set to try again in this year's Queen Anne, having come closest of all in his Lockinge battle with Rhododendron. The Aidan O'Brien-trained filly might stand in his way again and, even if she steps back up in trip for the Prince of Wales's Stakes instead, Simcock knows that elusive Group 1 victory will not come easily.

"If somebody could tell me where I'd find one, I'd be so happy," he said ruefully after the Lockinge body blow. "It's so frustrating, it really is."

Lightning Spear has twice won the Group 2 Celebration Mile at Goodwood, recording a Racing Post Rating of 119 for his first success in 2016 and 117 for his repeat victory last August. Fast summer ground seems to suit him well for that race, although Simcock does not see it as essential and Lightning Spear's third place to top US mare Tepin in the 2016 Queen Anne came on soft going.

His best RPR of 122 came in another of those Group 1 defeats when he was third to Minding in the 2016 Queen Elizabeth II Stakes at Ascot, with the ground given as good on that occasion. Simcock doubts he quite stays the stiff mile on the royal track and his record there (203396) is as frustrating as anywhere.

Many will expect him to fall short again but a breakthrough Group 1 triumph for such a gallant performer would be warmly welcomed, most especially at Simcock's yard. "We're very fond of him in the stable because we know him so well and he's a lovely horse to train," the trainer said. "He's very straightforward and my wife rides him every day and the kids feed him apples. He's that type of horse."

STAR RATING
★★★

'We're very fond of him in the stable because we know him so well and he's a lovely horse to train'

The future starts here

EXCITEMENT has been building around Crystal Ocean for 12 months or more but until now most of the talk has centred on those dreaded 'p' words: promise and potential. They can be the foundation stones of a great career but equally they can be the rocks on which hopes and dreams are dashed. Royal Ascot may give us the best indication yet of which way Crystal Ocean is heading.

Just over a year ago Crystal Ocean was being well backed for the Derby but then came defeat in the Dante at York and he did not go to Epsom. Instead he turned up at the royal meeting for the 'Ascot Derby', the King Edward VII Stakes, and was beaten favourite in third behind Permian, the Dante winner who had been tenth at Epsom in the meantime. So far, so ordinary.

Sir Michael Stoute gave the colt a six-week break and brought him back at Goodwood, where we saw a different Crystal Ocean. Well backed again, he took the Group 3 Gordon Stakes by three and a half lengths from Khalidi, reversing form emphatically with the King

*'He's got form
at ten and 12
furlongs. He's
consistent,
progressive
and versatile'*

Edward VII runner-up.

That earned him a place in one of the best St Legers for years and he acquitted himself admirably over a trip Stoute feels was stretching him, finishing a half-length runner-up to Capri. It was high-class form – Stradivarius, this year's impressive Yorkshire Cup winner, was third and

Melbourne Cup hero Rekindling was fourth – but still it is all about what Crystal Ocean might do in the future.

For now he is just a Group 3 winner, albeit a triple one after adding to his spoils this season in the Gordon Richards Stakes at Sandown and the Aston Park Stakes at Newbury. His six-length victory in the Aston Park, over what seems his optimum trip of 1m4f, demonstrated he was well beyond that level but he still needs to put that into black and white in the form book.

The obvious target at Royal Ascot is the Group 2 Hardwicke Stakes – a race won by Stoute on ten occasions – but a measure of

the regard in which Crystal Ocean is held is that he is also entered in the Group 1 Prince of Wales's Stakes over 1m2f, as well as the Eclipse at Sandown later on.

"He's got form at ten and 12 furlongs, but we're not going to decide where he's going to go yet as I don't know," Stoute said at Newbury.

"Consistent, progressive and versatile," were Stoute's chosen adjectives for Crystal Ocean after that success. The feeling remains that the master trainer will be describing him in much more glowing terms before too long.

STAR RATING
★★★★

Longer-range plan

HENRY CANDY'S project to turn 2016 July Cup winner Limato from a sprinter into a miler appeared to be derailed by a disappointing tenth place in the Lockinge Stakes at Newbury in May, but the trainer's inclination was to get back on track quickly and continue to head in the direction of the Queen Anne Stakes.

Limato has gained Group 1 success at 6f and 7f and finished second in the Commonwealth Cup and third in the Diamond Jubilee Stakes on his previous visits to Royal Ascot, but at a mile his form figures read 460.

Candy, though, believes the five-year-old is developing more into a miler with age. "He's in the Queen Anne and Diamond Jubilee and I think we'll probably persevere with the mile and ignore [the Lockinge] completely," he said after the Newbury setback.

The Oxfordshire trainer had a ready explanation for the poor performance in the Lockinge, in which Limato finished more than ten lengths behind Rhododendron, who was ante-post favourite for the Queen Anne after her win.

"We're surrounded by thousands of acres of oilseed rape and every plant and tree is in bloom," Candy said. "I think it affects horses' breathing to an extent. It happens every year. It just takes the edge off them. They travel all right until push comes to shove and then it just takes its toll a bit."

Limato will go to Royal Ascot with plenty to prove but on peak form he would be a serious contender if he stays the stiff mile. His best Racing Post Rating of 126 came over the intermediate distance of 7f in the 2016 Prix de la Foret and he was still capable of 123 over that trip in the Group 2 Challenge Stakes at Newmarket last October.

STAR RATING

★★★

Recovery mission

THIS strapping son of Wootton Bassett marked himself out as a miler of exceptional promise in two wide-margin wins as a juvenile, the second coming at Deauville in the same Listed race that threw up Al Wukair 12 months previously.

Godolphin had already purchased Wootton before that second success and the smiles around the winner's enclosure afterwards spoke of excitement for the future every bit as much as relief.

Alex Pantall's colt looked to have done well through the winter and held off Olmedo in a heavy-ground Prix de Fontainebleau on his comeback, before starting clear favourite in the Poule d'Essai des Poulains back at Longchamp a month later.

Everything that could go wrong in the Classic came to pass, with Wootton missing a beat out of the stalls before getting lit up when caught in the backwash of US Navy Flag's slip and bolting to the front. In the circumstances he did well to finish fourth, having done his running before Olmedo swept past to win.

Connections decided to put a line through the race and continue to back their belief Wootton is top class, though the electric atmosphere of Ascot could pose a challenge to his temperament.

Pantall is not a frequent visitor to Ascot but came close to pulling off the upset of all time when Restiadargent finished a head and a neck behind Black Caviar and Moonlight Cloud in the 2012 Diamond Jubilee Stakes.

Wootton would set off with far more serious pretensions of claiming success than that underrated challenger if Pantall makes the trip for the St James's Palace Stakes.

STAR RATING
★★★

Into the unknown

BIG ORANGE, last year's Gold Cup winner after an epic battle with Order Of St George, has been ruled out for the season but that doesn't mean life will be any easier for Ireland's top stayer as he tries to regain the crown he wore in 2016.

Chief among the fresh challengers to Order Of St George is Stradivarius, who threw down the gauntlet with an impressive victory in the Group 2 Yorkshire Cup in May. The John Gosden-trained four-year-old scored by three lengths from Desert Skyline with a dominant performance that confirmed him as an emerging force in the big staying races.

Victory at York also put Stradivarius in contention for the Weatherbys Hamilton Stayers' Million – the £1m prize if a horse wins one of the four staying prep races in May (of which the Yorkshire Cup was one) and goes on to take the Gold Cup, the Goodwood Cup in July and the Lonsdale Cup at York in August.

Gosden's colt had already advertised his strong claims as a stayer on the upgrade with victory over Big Orange in last year's Goodwood Cup and a close third behind Capri and Crystal Ocean in the St Leger, followed by another third place in the Long Distance Cup at Ascot in October. On that occasion he was beaten a length by Order Of St George, with Torcedor – another who is in line for the £1m – in between them.

The Yorkshire Cup is run over 1m6f and, unlike Order Of St George, Stradivarius will be heading into the unknown over the 2m4f of the Gold Cup.

"You can't practise a horse over two and a half miles at

home, so we'll find out whether he'll stay or not in the home straight at Ascot," Gosden said at York. "It's uncharted territory but he switches off and that will have taken the freshness out of him."

Bjorn Nielsen, owner-breeder of Stradivarius, is excited. "Having any kind of winner is great, and having a big winner and a horse to follow through the season is phenomenal. I'll be thinking of Stradivarius every day of the week this summer," he said.

"We won't find out whether he'll stay the Ascot Gold Cup trip until the day – it's impossible to tell. Some of the best two-milers haven't stayed the extra distance, but we'll soon find out."

STAR RATING
★★★★

Owner: BE Nielsen
Trainer: John Gosden

'We won't find out whether he'll stay the Ascot Gold Cup trip until the day – it's impossible to tell. Some of the best two-milers haven't stayed the extra distance, but we'll soon find out'

Speed machine

LAST year Sioux Nation was a 14-1 winner for Aidan O'Brien in the Norfolk Stakes but he is hotly fancied this time after a scintillating warm-up in the Group 3 Lacken Stakes at Naas.

That was the same prep Caravaggio was given by O'Brien before his victory over Harry Angel in the Group 1 Commonwealth Cup 12 months ago and the sprint for three-year-olds looks set to be the target with Sioux Nation, although the open-age King's Stand Stakes over 5f – a furlong shorter than the Lacken and the Commonwealth Cup – remains on the table.

"We came here to find out if it was five or six [furlongs that he wanted] at Royal Ascot and Seamus [Heffernan, on Fleet Review] went along in front to make it a proper test," O'Brien said at Naas.

"We always felt he had a lot of speed and we wanted to see whether we'd go for the King's Stand Stakes or the Commonwealth Cup."

And the view from Ryan Moore in the saddle? "Ryan said he has all the speed in the world and that he'd have no problem going back to five furlongs, but maybe let him take on the three-year-olds [at Royal Ascot] and then look forward to the Nunthorpe. That's what Ryan said anyway."

Sioux Nation had already run, and won, over 6f early last season before he dropped back to the minimum trip to win the Norfolk. Then he went back up to 6f and scored a Group 1 victory by half a length over Beckford in the Phoenix Stakes at the Curragh in August.

Beckford, then trained by Gordon Elliott and now in

Owner: Michael Tabor, Derrick Smith & Sue Magnier
Trainer: Aidan O'Brien

'Ryan said he has all the speed in the world and that he'd have no problem going back to five furlongs, but maybe let him take on the three-year-olds [at Royal Ascot] and then look forward to the Nunthorpe'

the US with Brendan Walsh, is a potential rival in the Commonwealth Cup, but he might struggle to keep tabs on Sioux Nation this time judging by the blistering pace O'Brien's flyer showed in the Lacken. Indeed, there might be quite a few who find themselves gasping for air.

Interestingly, the Norfolk and Phoenix were both run on good to firm ground and

the Lacken was the first time Sioux Nation had encountered such fast conditions since the Phoenix.

"He's a great traveller and he quickened well," O'Brien said. "The ground couldn't be fast enough for him – fast ground, fast horse."

STAR RATING
★★★★

TOP HORSES

SOUTHERN FRANCE

Aidan O'Brien has won three of the last five runnings of the Queen's Vase – albeit before the race distance was cut last year from 2m to 1m6f – and he could have a live contender with Southern France.

The strapping son of Galileo did not make his first racecourse appearance until April but three quick runs took him to Listed success over 1m5f at Navan, with jockey Donnacha O'Brien saying: "I wanted to make it into a bit of a test. He stays well and the Queen's Vase could be a natural next step."

TOMYRIS

Last year French raider Qemah finished second in the Group 3 Chartwell Fillies' Stakes at Lingfield in May before landing the Duke of Cambridge Stakes at the royal meeting and that Group 2 mile for older fillies and mares is the target for this year's Chartwell winner, the Roger Varian-trained Tomyris. She was only sixth in last year's Coronation Stakes – a race Qemah won in 2016 – but could be a typical Varian late developer.

WIND CHIMES

Andre Fabre does not send runners to Royal Ascot without serious intent and

his unlucky third from the French 1,000 Guineas would be one to consider if she is on his team in the Coronation Stakes. The Coolmore-owned filly had been mentioned as a Newmarket Guineas possible before she was kept back for her home version, in which she finished fast from a wide draw in a rough race to be beaten a short neck and a head behind Teppal.

Six more to watch

'This Aidan O'Brien-trained colt is the type who could end up at Royal Ascot after being on the Derby trail, having been third in the Feilden Stakes at Newmarket and then second in the Lingfield Derby Trial'

2016 Across The Stars was third at Lingfield before winning the King Edward VII Stakes, having finished tenth in the Derby in between.

HEARTACHE

Clive Cox's flying filly won the Queen Mary Stakes at last year's royal meeting and later added another Group 2 success over 5f in the Flying Childers at Doncaster, giving her the right profile for a crack at the Group 1 Commonwealth Cup. Cox, who has enjoyed great success with sprinters, has told the Racing Post: "I'm excited about her. She has a great physical appearance and I firmly believe she'll get 6f well as a three-year-old."

WADILSAFA

Owen Burrows may not have had a Royal Ascot winner of his own but he knows what it takes, having spent 13 years as assistant to Sir Michael Stoute, and believes Wadilsafa could be the right type. The three-year-old won a mile novice at Newmarket on his reappearance and Burrows, who became private trainer to Hamdan Al Maktoum in 2016, said: "Once he hit the rising ground he came home good. He looks a big, strong galloper and the Hampton Court could be a nice race for him."

KEW GARDENS

This Aidan O'Brien-trained colt *(above)* is the type who could end up at Royal Ascot after being on the Derby trail, having been third in the Feilden Stakes at Newmarket and then second in the Lingfield Derby Trial. Last year's first four from the Lingfield race ran at the royal meeting – albeit without showing much – and in

TOP HORSES

SERGEI PROKOFIEV

Aidan O'Brien always has a hot prospect for the juvenile races and this son of Scat Daddy – the late sire who supplied four Royal Ascot winners last year – has been the one to set the Coventry Stakes ante-post market alight, although he has yet to race beyond 5f. He was green on his first start at Dundalk and lost out to a more experienced rival, but how O'Brien's juveniles perform on debut often proves no guide to what they might go on to achieve. Sergei Prokofiev duly stepped up second time to score by seven and a half lengths at Navan and on his third run at Naas the margin was four lengths. "He's very natural and gets there very easy," O'Brien said at Naas. "It'll be either the Coventry or Norfolk and that will depend on what we do with some of the other two-year-olds."

BLOWN BY WIND

Mark Johnston is another trainer who always has a strong team of two-year-olds and the 2018 bunch includes this son of Invincible Spirit, who made it two wins out of three with a 5f victory at Ascot. He is set to go for the 6f Coventry, with Johnston saying at Ascot: "We felt that was a clear indication Blown By Wind would be more comfortable over 6f. In the shadow of the post he's finding another gear." Among the other Johnston juveniles to note are I Am A Dreamer and No Lippy.

ADVERTISE

Martyn Meade, now based at the historic Manton training estate in Wiltshire, was bullish after this son of Showcasing rewarded strong market support with a debut victory over 6f at Newbury. "He didn't get backed into favourite without people thinking he was quite a good horse," he said. "It was the way he did it, settling in last

Six two-year-olds to watch

and then being produced. For me that's a pretty good horse. If you win these races, Royal Ascot is the next thing. I wouldn't be hesitant about it and this horse will go straight there."

WEDDING DATE

With Royal Ascot set to bask in the afterglow of the marriage of Prince Harry and Meghan Markle, this could be a popular filly among racegoers – and trainer Richard Hannon wasn't putting anyone off after her second-time-out win at Chester. "It was a massive improvement from her first run but she didn't come down the hill at Brighton.

She definitely looked to have black-type potential the way she won," he said.

SIGNORA CABELLO

Four years ago The Wow Signal stormed away with the Coventry Stakes for John Quinn and the North Yorkshire trainer has another flyer in Signora Cabello *(left, winning)*, who is already a Listed winner after taking the Marygate Stakes at York – a significant Queen Mary prep – to make it two wins from three starts. "She won well and we've always liked her," Quinn said. "We thought she'd hose up on her debut but it all went against her on the day, then she won a hot race at Bath. She's got a very good pedigree and we'll go for the Queen Mary – it's the obvious race to go for."

CHARMING KID

Richard Fahey has had only one juvenile winner at Royal Ascot – Marine Commando in the 2010 Windsor Castle Stakes – but he has a good prospect in this son of Charm Spirit. The £105,000 breeze-up purchase made a winning debut over 5f at York that earned an instant quote of 8-1 for the Norfolk Stakes over the same trip. "I'd be thinking of the Norfolk," Fahey said. "He's quite sharp and you need plenty of boot at Ascot."

THE INTERNATIONAL CHALLENGE

Nicholas Godfrey traces Royal Ascot's growth into a global race meeting

D O you remember the days before Choisir? Royal Ascot was a different place then – quite literally, as the old stands were still there. None of us had heard of Wesley Ward, while the idea of a Kentucky Derby winner coming to run at Britain's greatest meeting would have been met with howls of derision.

The racing world was changing fast, however, and the sport was increasingly cosmopolitan, with the idea of horses travelling across continents no longer just a bit of potentially lucrative end-of-season colour confined to the Breeders' Cup, or maybe the Japan Cup and Hong Kong.

For all its heritage, status and prestige, Britain was in severe danger of getting left behind as a parochial affair. Until Royal Ascot took up the charge, that is, and Australian sprint pioneer Choisir kicked down the door with that unforgettable King's Stand Stakes/Golden

'We have worked to attract horses from all over the world'

Jubilee double within five days in 2003. Without Choisir's efforts, it is not fanciful to suggest there might have been no Takeover Target, no Black Caviar, maybe no Lady Aurelia nor Tepin.

Not so long ago, the prospect of an American trainer habitually running lightning-fast juveniles on a strip of Berkshire turf would have been laughed out of court but Ward, Royal Ascot's favourite adopted son, is a permanent fixture now and long-range visitors are part and parcel of the royal meeting's landscape, having added to its lustre for a decade and a half with an array of world-class horses.

"It is increasingly important for Ascot to remain at the forefront of the international racing community," says Nick Smith, Ascot's director of racing and communications. "We have worked to attract horses from all over the

world, principally for profile and reputational reasons but these days the benefits are far more wide-reaching.

"For example, the consistent success of Wesley Ward's team from the US led to the star Breeders' Cup winner Tepin's successful and ground-breaking win in the Queen Anne and that in turn led to NBC's considerably increased interest in Royal Ascot. This year they will once again cover the event extensively, almost in full, including inserts into the Today programme on the main channel, with much more on-site presence than ever before."

Smith has become a familiar face on the world stage in his role as the meeting's international recruiter and barely a decent Group 1 race goes by anywhere on the planet without his attempting to lure the winning connections.

It doesn't always work, of course, but even the biggest sceptic would be forced to admit that a number of the most memorable episodes in

'We had nine nations represented a few years back'

recent Royal Ascot history have come courtesy of the transcontinental horses.

"Every year is different," explains Smith. "Last year's theme was American, in terms of competition from outside Europe; there were a record 14 runners and five stables represented including, for the first time, Bill Mott. The serious names in the US are definitely taking notice, while also, of course, being realistic about the task – you need a serious champion to win a Royal Ascot Group 1.

"In some years the story has been variety," Smith goes on. "We had nine nations represented a few years back. Australians have been crucial over a period of time and there have been five sprint winners including Choisir, who changed world racing and perceptions about what could be done, and of course Black Caviar, who made her sole overseas foray to Royal Ascot." ▶

New dawn: Choisir (right) heads to victory in the 2003 King's Stand Stakes

THE INTERNATIONAL CHALLENGE

Admittedly, it isn't cheap and it isn't easy – just look at the Japanese record; they've yet to get a horse placed – and it's not always been plain sailing. These are horses we're talking about, after all, and there have been severe disappointments, none more so than three years ago when American Horse of the Year California Chrome was ruled out on the eve of the meeting with a bruised foot. His compatriot Animal Kingdom's abject display in the Queen Anne in 2013 was another low point, as was the dismal failure of Hong Kong superstar Able Friend in the same contest two years later.

The good days, though, have been really good – and one in particular stands out for Smith. No prizes for guessing which one. "Nothing can ever compare to the Black Caviar effect," says Smith, vividly remembering the fateful visit of Australia's favourite horse for the Diamond Jubilee in 2012.

"The week had started with a frenzy with Frankel's Queen Anne win but there was a sense that everything was always building up to Black Caviar.

"I've never seen anything like the sea of salmon pink and black flags, ties, everything you can imagine. Not many horses have Federation Square [in Melbourne] packed with 12,000 people to watch their hero on a big screen at gone midnight, but Black Caviar did. It was like the whole world was taking a collective gulp as the race began, and the rest is history."

Black Caviar fever: Royal Ascot had never seen anything like the scenes that unfolded in 2012

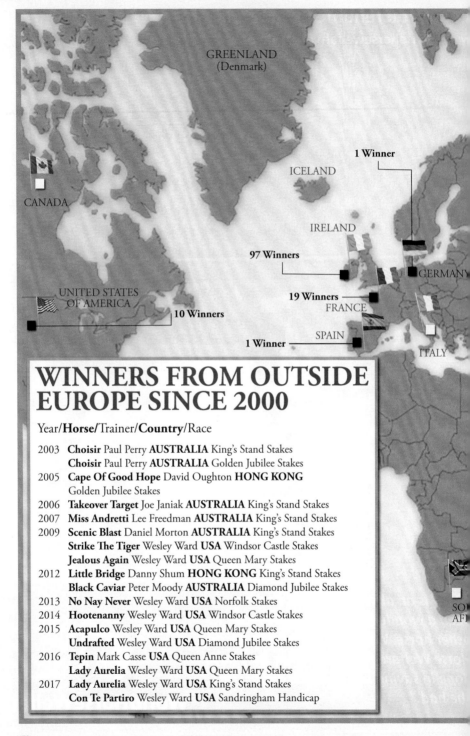

GREENLAND
(Denmark)

ICELAND

1 Winner

CANADA

IRELAND

97 Winners

GERMANY

UNITED STATES
OF AMERICA

19 Winners
FRANCE

10 Winners

1 Winner

SPAIN

ITALY

SO
AF

WINNERS FROM OUTSIDE EUROPE SINCE 2000

Year/**Horse**/Trainer/**Country**/Race

2003   **Choisir** Paul Perry **AUSTRALIA** King's Stand Stakes
       Choisir Paul Perry **AUSTRALIA** Golden Jubilee Stakes
2005   **Cape Of Good Hope** David Oughton **HONG KONG**
       Golden Jubilee Stakes
2006   **Takeover Target** Joe Janiak **AUSTRALIA** King's Stand Stakes
2007   **Miss Andretti** Lee Freedman **AUSTRALIA** King's Stand Stakes
2009   **Scenic Blast** Daniel Morton **AUSTRALIA** King's Stand Stakes
       Strike The Tiger Wesley Ward **USA** Windsor Castle Stakes
       Jealous Again Wesley Ward **USA** Queen Mary Stakes
2012   **Little Bridge** Danny Shum **HONG KONG** King's Stand Stakes
       Black Caviar Peter Moody **AUSTRALIA** Diamond Jubilee Stakes
2013   **No Nay Never** Wesley Ward **USA** Norfolk Stakes
2014   **Hootenanny** Wesley Ward **USA** Windsor Castle Stakes
2015   **Acapulco** Wesley Ward **USA** Queen Mary Stakes
       Undrafted Wesley Ward **USA** Diamond Jubilee Stakes
2016   **Tepin** Mark Casse **USA** Queen Anne Stakes
       Lady Aurelia Wesley Ward **USA** Queen Mary Stakes
2017   **Lady Aurelia** Wesley Ward **USA** King's Stand Stakes
       Con Te Partiro Wesley Ward **USA** Sandringham Handicap

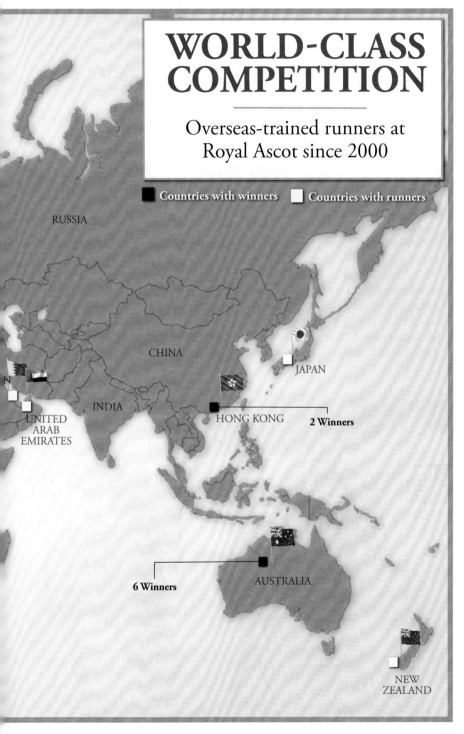

WORLD-CLASS COMPETITION

Overseas-trained runners at Royal Ascot since 2000

■ Countries with winners   □ Countries with runners

RUSSIA

CHINA

JAPAN

UNITED
ARAB
EMIRATES

INDIA

HONG KONG   2 Winners

AUSTRALIA

6 Winners

NEW
ZEALAND

Cross-channel aces

The French raiding party usually numbers around 20 runners and the quality is so high – and their strike-rate so good – that they are impossible to ignore.

There has been at least one French-trained winner at 11 of the 17 Royal Ascots since 2000 and the challenge from the other side of the English Channel has diversified and strengthened in recent years, with a greater number of trainers prepared to send runners to the meeting.

Last year France had three winners from 16 runners, following on from two (from 18) the year before and three (from 19) in 2015. Overall, in the past three years, the strike-rate is 15 per cent for a level-stake profit of +6.19pt.

Despite that profit figure, backing blind is not the best policy and there are more nuanced ways of making money on French runners.

One is to be price-sensitive and concentrate only on runners who are well fancied in the betting market. By definition, those are the runners with the best form and it is notable that four of the seven French winners in the past three years went off favourite.

Not only that, but that

French trainers

quartet were the only French-trained outright favourites in the past three years, producing a 100 per cent strike-rate and a level-stake profit of +8.13pt.

Overall, since 2000, eight of the 17 French-trained outright favourites have

Le Brivido (facing page, left) wins last year's Jersey Stakes for Andre Fabre (above); Qemah (above) lands the 2017 Duke of Cambridge Stakes for Jean-Claude Rouget; Solow scorches home for France in the 2015 Queen Anne Stakes

been successful (47%, +6.64pt).

Another way of narrowing down the French challenge is to focus on the fillies. Four of their seven winners in the past three years came in races restricted to fillies and mares (22%, +13.75pt) and perhaps that is because these divisions lack some depth and French trainers send only their best-regarded fillies.

On the trainer front, Andre Fabre always has to be respected (two winners, a second and a third from eight runners in the past five years) and Jean-Claude Rouget is similarly strong now (three winners and a second from eight runners in the same period).

OUTRIGHT FAVOURITES HAVE HIGH STRIKE-RATE

TOP TIPS

STRONG RECORD IN FILLIES-ONLY RACES

US speedball is back

BLINK and you'll miss her: Lady Aurelia is back again bidding for a hat-trick at the head of the usual formidable Royal Ascot team for the meeting's adopted American son Wesley Ward.

Few horses have scorched the famous Berkshire turf like the four-year-old daughter of Scat Daddy, whose astonishing seven-length victory in the Queen Mary Stakes as a two-year-old remains indelibly printed on the collective Ascot memory. Then came more of the same 12 months ago – albeit by only three lengths – in the King's Stand Stakes, the race that once again provides her target. A third victory would put her in an elite club of nine horses who have achieved that number or more at Royal Ascot in the past half-century.

Something is different this time around, however, as Lady Aurelia comes into the meeting on the back of a surprise defeat on her seasonal debut in Listed company at Keeneland in April. "She's an older-season mare now and had been training very well coming into the race," says Ward, who has saddled nine Royal Ascot winners since his first sortie in 2009. "However, looking at the race afterwards and with hindsight, she was racing against fillies who were race-fit and had been running throughout the winter. They were tough, hardy and fit horses, while Lady Aurelia was only just starting to come back into work.

"Also, that race was over five and a half furlongs and she's a real out-and-out five-furlong horse – that's the trip at which she's most effective. Watching that race again, she was in front at five furlongs, so if the race had been over a flat five furlongs, we would have won. The winner only put that extra kick in to score over the last half-furlong."

Ward was encouraged by Lady Aurelia's work after the Keeneland contest. "Last year, working into the Breeders' Cup, I thought she was getting complacent, kinda easy-going, taking things in stride. For whatever reason, she went out to Del Mar and didn't fire and maybe that was a telltale sign that she wasn't relaxed and doing things on her own.

"Now she's really aggressive like she has been in the past.

Owner: Stonestreet Stables & Peter Leidel
Trainer: Wesley Ward

That's what you want to see going to where we've been a couple of times before. There are some very good sprinters in England right now, but I'm confident she can win the race again. She's so talented and given that she's a bigger and stronger filly this year, I think she'll take all the beating."

Lady Aurelia will be accompanied by a powerful team from the Ward barn, including Bound For Nowhere, who will also run in the King's Stand; he ran a sound race in 2017 when fourth in a red-hot Commonwealth Cup. Hemp Hemp Hurray is the Ward contender for the three-year-old contest this time around, though he has the Jersey Stakes as an alternative.

Of course, Ward's juveniles are always to be feared. Among those earmarked for Ascot this year are Chelsea Cloisters (Queen Mary), Shang Shang Shang (Norfolk) and Stillwater Cove (Albany).

STAR RATING
★★★★★

Back on home turf

THERE is nothing even vaguely unusual about a horse who was unbeaten in a pair of starts as a three-year-old for William Haggas making up into the sort of high-class performer who might appear in his later years at Royal Ascot.

Little else, though, about Redkirk Warrior's journey from Newmarket to the royal meeting has been entirely straightforward. Now a seven-year-old gelding, he has had an unconventional career path and arrives back in Blighty after a rather circuitous journey to Australia via Hong Kong.

A 22,000gns yearling, he was known initially simply as 'Redkirk' in Britain, where he won over 1m2f at Yarmouth and Ascot before being a beaten favourite in the Hong Kong Derby and finally converted into a top sprinter down

under for the Lindsay Park training partnership of David Hayes, son Ben and nephew Tom Dabernig.

A shock 30-1 winner of the prestigious Newmarket Handicap in 2017, he completed back-to-back victories in the historic Group 1 event at Flemington in March, making a lot of the running under top weight on the stands rail – three weeks after a stunning last-to-first victory in the Black Caviar Lightning Stakes, beating Everest winner Redzel over five furlongs.

Local experience means Frankie Dettori takes over from regular rider Regan Bayliss at Ascot. "I saw David in Dubai and he told me he had a nice sprinter for me to ride at Ascot," says Dettori. "It's exciting as he's a triple Group 1 winner – and one thing the Australians are definitely good at is sprinters."

Redkirk Warrior, set to be housed at Jane Chapple-Hyam's

Newmarket yard, is charged with ending a relative drought for Australian sprinters at Royal Ascot. After a period of dominance sparked by Choisir's double strike in 2003, none has struck since Black Caviar in 2012.

"It's on my bucket list to train a winner in the UK," says Melbourne Cup-winning trainer David Hayes, who has more than 4,000 winners to his name – among them 90-plus Group 1 victories.

"I've had a couple of tries with Nicconi and Criterion, but if you go to England you should go with what you're good at, and for us that's sprinters, even though he's a Pom himself really. Hopefully he'll be fit for a queen."

Although the Diamond Jubilee is Redkirk Warrior's primary target, a bad weather forecast could prompt a switch, according to co-trainer Dabernig. "His wet-track form isn't as good as his dry-track form, so we're keeping all options open, but the intention is to run on the Saturday," he explains.

STAR RATING
★★★★

Owner: MB Lee & Miss YCJ Tam
Trainer: David & Ben Hayes & Tom Dabernig

'It's on my bucket list to train a winner in the UK. If you go to England you should go with what you're good at, and for us that's sprinters'

The Irish American

THE horse's name will be familiar, having figured prominently in a string of top juvenile contests in Ireland last year for Gordon Elliott, but the identity of his new trainer will be less well known to British and Irish racing fans.

Both Beckford and Brendan Walsh left Ireland to make their fortune in the United States, and now they are set to return together for an assault on the Group 1 Commonwealth Cup at Royal Ascot.

Walsh, originally from County Cork but now training in Kentucky, took over the training of Beckford from Elliott after the colt had finished fifth to Mendelssohn in the Breeders' Cup Juvenile Turf at Del Mar. That completed a juvenile campaign which featured a Group 2 victory in the Railway Stakes and a pair of Group 1 second places in the Phoenix and National Stakes, all at the Curragh.

Walsh was quick off the mark with Beckford when he sent him out for a reappearance win in a 5f stakes race at Churchill Downs in April and he is optimistic about the task ahead.

"I'm really excited to be going back over there. He's got a lovely temperament and I would think he'll handle it all really well," he says.

"I think he's got a lot of natural speed. Last year in Europe he was up there with the best of them and he looks like he has retained that form, if not improved. That alone should make him competitive.

"He showed a great turn of foot and did everything right when winning on his debut for me. It was a bit of an adjustment for him, dropping back to five furlongs, and I think he'll improve a lot.

"The nice thing about taking him all the way over there is that he's not ground dependent – I think he'll go on anything. It certainly wasn't lightning fast at Churchill Downs as they'd had a lot of rain a few days before."

Walsh, 45, started training in his own right six years ago and now has around 40 horses. He worked for Godolphin for ten years and was assistant to Mark Wallace in Newmarket before heading off to pursue his American dream, first as assistant to Eddie Kenneally.

He recalls a near miss at the royal meeting from his time with Wallace. "My greatest Ascot memory was when Benbaun got beaten a short head by Takeover Target in the King's Stand in 2006. That was a good day, but not a great day," he says.

With Beckford as his representative, Walsh is hoping to go one better on the grandest of stages.

STAR RATING
★★★

Owner: Newtown Anner Stud Farm
Trainer: Brendan Walsh

'Last year in Europe
he was up there with
the best of them and
he looks like he has
retained that form, if
not improved'

'It's on our bucket list'

"NO sheikhs or billionaires need apply" goes their motto, but the US-based Ironhorse Racing Stable are looking forward to mixing with royalty when Bucchero runs in the King's Stand Stakes.

The six-year-old, who is trained by Kentucky-based Tim Glyshaw, is one of the leading turf sprinters in North America, having been a close fourth in last year's Breeders' Cup Turf Sprint before finishing second to probable King's Stand Stakes rival Bound For Nowhere at Keeneland in April and a luckless third on his final Royal Ascot prep at Churchill Downs in Grade 3 company.

"We were very happy with the way he ran [at Churchill Downs] – we just weren't particularly pleased with the severe bump he received just as he was about to make the lead coming out of the turn," says Harlan Malter, managing director of her owners Ironhorse Racing.

"However, what we're most proud of and really what makes Bucchero so special is that even with the bump, when many horses would have quit, he put his head down, pinned his ears

and went about trying to win the race despite the trouble. Knowing his career and backstory, this should not come as a surprise."

Indeed not. Bred far away from the bright lights in Indiana, Bucchero is out of a dam, Meetmeontime, who was rescued by the Marion County Humane Society in the summer of 2009 when she was found among 33 neglected horses on a farm in Ocala, Florida. Restored to full health, she went on

> 'This horse is a really cool customer. Every time he has been to a new track he eats, settles down and sleeps'

to produce five foals, the second of whom was Bucchero.

"I think Bucchero has run at 13 tracks in 27 races, which is obviously more common in Europe but pretty rare over here in the US," adds Malter. "This horse is a really cool customer. Every time he has been to a new track he eats,

settles down and sleeps. He takes it all in his stride. It's pretty amazing."

Malter's syndicate are self-proclaimed 'ordinary Joes' – hence that line about sheikhs and billionaires on their website.

"The game is now played at a very elite level as far as horses and ownership goes," explains Malter, whose 'day job' is financial planning. "But the majority of the fans across the world are everyday people who love racing with a passion and have a true love of the horses.

"There have been some amazing rags-to-riches horse stories and I've always been drawn to these horses," he adds.

"There are four other partners in the horse and we'll all be coming over to Ascot; we're all great sports fans and to have a runner at Royal Ascot was on our bucket list.

"To have a horse who can come over to Royal Ascot with a chance is rarer than a [Kentucky] Derby horse and we all recognise how lucky we are to have a horse who will get us there."

STAR RATING
★★★

FIVE OF THE BEST . . .

CAFFE FEGO

Breakfast is the most important meal of the day, so they say, and that is even more true before a day of punting, drinking and wearing fancy dress. Caffe Fego, located all of a third of a mile from the main gates on the High Street, is the ideal space. The breakfast menu ranges from spicy scrambled eggs to breakfast burritos, via traditional fry-ups. Whatever you opt for will surely go with one of their breakfast cocktails.

1768 GRILL & TEA ROOMS

If surf and turf is your thing, this is the place for you. Located in the Queen Anne Enclosure, it's Ascot's largest walk-up restaurant during the royal meeting and the menu is as hearty as the square footage.

Steak, lobster and seafood platters are on the menu as well as traditional afternoon tea later on if that's more your thing. And let's face it, at an occasion like Royal Ascot of course it's your thing.

Places to eat

SIMON ROGAN

If you're lucky enough to be in the Royal Enclosure you could always have one of the world's leading chefs cook for you. The Michelin-starred culinary genius that is Simon Rogan – yes, he of L'Enclume and Roganic fame – is cooking for the first time at the royal meeting at a new walk-up restaurant and promises "some really exciting seasonal menus featuring the best British produce". A winner or two might come in handy for paying the bill.

SUSSEX CHARMER

If you've done nothing but back losers all day and need a tasty treat to lift your spirits, you're in luck with this reliable favourite. Just £6 is all you need for this mouthful of deliciousness. Located by the bandstand, Sussex dairy farmers Bookham & Harrison melt their product into gooey goodness that's so tasty you'll leave with a smile on your face even if you've made six shocking decisions in the betting ring.

LA SORRENTINA

You'll struggle to do better than La Sorrentina if you're looking for an after-racing bite to eat while letting the traffic or train queues ease. Two miles from the racecourse and a few strides over a mile's walk from the train station, this little gem in Sunninghill is ideal whatever your chosen mode of transport. La Sorrentina combines an authentic home-cooked flavour and family-run Italian vibe to make a delightful end to the day.

FIVE OF THE BEST . . .

GRUNDY & BUSTINO BAR

Named after the two stars of what is widely considered the greatest race of all time, the 1975 King George, this bar and kitchen offers a tranquil lawn on which to enjoy fine wines alongside a range of food. Located in the Queen Anne Enclosure, the bar overlooks the pre-parade ring, ensuring guests are able to keep an eye on the racing as they enjoy their lunch.

JAGZ

Whether it be for a champagne breakfast, a quick pint before heading up to the course or a post-racing after-party to celebrate going through the card, Jagz has it all. Right next to the station, Jagz is a vibrant venue consisting of the Station Inn, a live music stage and a nightclub. You can dance the night away – well, until 11pm on weeknights or midnight on Friday and Saturday.

STAG PUB

This lively pub is in an ideal location just a few hundred yards from the entrance to the course and a short walk from the station. Serving a wide selection of beers, wines, champagnes and soft drinks, the Stag also has a large beer garden where you can soak up some sunshine and swap tales of punting glory or woe. The atmosphere makes it a fantastic place to start or finish your day.

Places to drink

BRIGADIER GERARD BAR

Located adjacent to the unsaddling enclosure, this is the perfect place to enjoy some refreshments while feeling right at the heart of the racing. It's shaded, there is usually a chair or two free, and you're right next to the horses when they go out to the track and when they come back. Plus there's a big screen in case you don't make it to the stands to watch the action.

DANCING BRAVE BAR

Named in homage to the outstanding horse of the 1986 Flat season, this bar is something of a star itself with its range of real ales, courtesy of Goose Island and Windsor and Eton Breweries. Located within the grandstand, the bar is accessible to Royal Enclosure and Queen Anne Enclosure guests and offers the chance to sample something a little different from the standard beers.

FIVE OF THE BEST . . .

THE ROYAL PROCESSION

It is the ultimate 'if your name's not on the list, you're not coming in'. Languidly anonymous aristocrats may get a seat in one of the four carriages each day, lavishly braided stalwarts of the armed forces have a chance, and Meghan Markle should be a shoo-in this summer. Now and again, a racing politico or a favoured high-end trainer may get the nod for the trip of a lifetime. But the rest of us will always be on the outside, looking in.

THE ROYAL ENCLOSURE

If you can't get an invite to the royal procession, the next best option is to join the privileged few who have access to a host of private facilities including the superb restaurants, bars and vantage points on the fourth floor of the grandstand. To become a member, you have to be sponsored by two existing members who have attended the Royal Enclosure for a minimum of five years, or you can go as a member's guest.

NO1 CAR PARK

It doesn't sound grand, does it? But it is one of the most treasured pieces of real estate in Berkshire, reserved for use by Royal Enclosure members and their guests (along with Car Parks 2 and 7). Picnicking in No1 Car Park – and we're talking the full works, with butlers, candelabra and silver service not uncommon – is a long-standing tradition held dear by berth-holders, who number around 1,300. There is a waiting list of 400 names.

Exclusive places

PARADE RING RESTAURANT

Ascot describes this as "the most prestigious of our restaurants" and no wonder – it sits opposite the royal box on level two of the grandstand, with private viewing areas overlooking the parade ring and the winning post. Each of the five courses on the menu is paired with a different champagne, and there is afternoon tea and a complimentary bar. Gold Cup day is £2,009 (plus VAT) with Saturday a relative bargain at £1,379 (plus VAT).

THE HELIPAD

There is more than one luxurious way to arrive at Royal Ascot – the Roller or Bentley might suffice – but climbing out of a helicopter is quite a status statement, especially if it's a private one. Ascot has an official partner offering a helicopter service from two locations, north or south of Ascot, located close to motorways. At £395 return, it is described as "the ultimate park and ride service" with the promise to whisk clients by car from the helipad to the grandstands in minutes.

DID YOU KNOW?

Royal Ascot racegoers consume 240,000 hand-crafted afternoon tea cakes, 60,000 finger sandwiches, 25,000 spears of English asparagus, 8,000 Cornish crabs, 7,000 punnets of mixed berries, 5,000kg of salmon, 5,000 Angus steaks and 1,200kg of Cornish clotted cream

Leader of the pack

Aidan O'Brien is the dominant force at Royal Ascot, just as he is across most of the Flat racing year, and he was crowned top trainer at the meeting for an eighth time in 2017 with six winners. It was the third win in succession for the Ballydoyle wizard and his fifth since 2011. For the purposes of this analysis we will concentrate on the period since 2010.

A stunning 33 of O'Brien's 61 Royal Ascot winners have come in that timeframe and he shares the post-war record of seven wins (2016) at one meeting with Sir Henry Cecil. The lion's share of those 33 wins have come in Group 1s, with 11 wins from 65 runners equating to a tidy 17 per cent strike-rate.

O'Brien's total ratio in weight-for-age Group and Listed races is 31-167 at a highly efficient 19 per cent and it rises accordingly as you go down the Pattern rankings. His yield in Listed races is greatest at 6-22 (27%) for a whopping +29.11pt level-stake profit,

MOST SUCCESSFUL RACES

Coventry Stakes
■■■■■■■■

Gold Cup
■■■■■■■

St James's Palace Stakes
■■■■■■■

Queen's Vase
■■■■■

Chesham Stakes
■■■■

Coronation Stakes
■■■

Hardwicke Stakes
■■■

Jersey Stakes
■■■

Norfolk Stakes
■■■

Prince of Wales's Stakes
■■■

Queen Anne Stakes
■■■

while it drops to 20 per cent in Group 3s and 18 per cent in Group 2s.

His return is just 2-19 (11%) in handicaps since 2010 and, while you would break even at that, he has become more prolific in the handicap realm lately, with his two wins coming from nine runners since 2015. Both were the only runners in their respective races and

were ridden by Ryan Moore, returning SPs of 7-1 and 10-1 (+10pt yield). Moore had just five rides in handicaps for O'Brien in that timeframe, with one other placed at 7-1.

It is slightly more unexpected that, of the eight O'Brien winners to return a double-figure SP since 2010, Moore was aboard three, as was Seamie Heffernan. Of those eight, four came in juvenile races, including two of the last three Norfolk Stakes (Waterloo Bridge at 12-1 and Sioux Nation at 14-1) when the winner was the stable's only representative and was ridden by Moore. O'Brien has had only seven runners in the Norfolk since 2010, and never more than one a year, so a +21pt return is significant.

The Britannia Handicap is another race he targets selectively, with his one

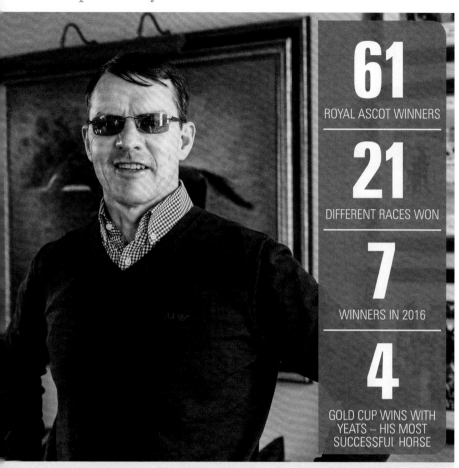

61

ROYAL ASCOT WINNERS

21

DIFFERENT RACES WON

7

WINNERS IN 2016

4

GOLD CUP WINS WITH YEATS – HIS MOST SUCCESSFUL HORSE

winner from three runners returned at 10-1.

None of his double-figure winners came in a Group 1, so the market tends to have a good handle on the pecking order at the elite end. That is reaffirmed by his yield with favourites. Of the 46 he has saddled, 19 have won (+5.9pt) for a 41 per cent strike-rate, and it

O'BRIEN'S WINNERS BY AGE GROUP

- 2yo **17**
- 3yo **25**
- 4yo+ **19**

doesn't drop if you factor in joint-favourites (20-49).

While O'Brien has saddled winners at every distance on the 30-race programme since 2010, 6f events have yielded the largest volume with six in all. He has won four of the five races at that trip since 2010 – the Wokingham (just one runner) being the exception.

The record chaser

No trainer can boast a longer stay at the helm of British Flat racing than Sir Michael Stoute and the ten-time champion stands on the brink of another major milestone, requiring just one more victory to take the outright record for Royal Ascot winners.

Stoute's score stands at 75 and he shares top spot with the late, great Sir Henry Cecil, having drawn level when Dartmouth won the Hardwicke Stakes on the final day of the 2016 meeting. He was frustrated in his quest for the 76th winner last year, going closest when Mori was beaten just a neck in the Ribblesdale Stakes.

The Newmarket trainer's first Royal Ascot winner came in the 1977 Jersey Stakes with Etienne Gerard, five years after he had started training, and his record has been a model of consistency. He has been top trainer at the meeting six times and 2017 marked just his seventh blank in the 41 years since his first success.

The winners have slowed

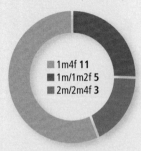

STOUTE'S WINNERS BY DISTANCE (2008-)

- ■ 1m4f **11**
- ■ 1m/1m2f **5**
- ■ 2m/2m4f **3**

in recent years, however. In the past decade he has had 19 winners, whereas the previous ten years brought 27 victories, and his only Group 1 success since 2003 was the Gold Cup with the Queen's Estimate in 2013.

The bulk of those recent winners have come in just five races – the Hardwicke (five), the Duke of Edinburgh Handicap (three) and the Queen's Vase, Duke of Cambridge

Snow Sky wins the 2015 Hardwicke Stakes – one of ten wins in the race for Stoute

Stakes and King Edward VII Stakes (two apiece) – and it would be no surprise if Stoute took the outright record with another victory in one of those contests.

What is notable about those favourite races is that four of the five are run at 1m4f-plus. The exception is the Duke of Cambridge Stakes over a mile, although that race is for fillies and mares – a department where Stoute also tends to be well stocked (Mori's near-miss last year was in the Group 2 Ribblesdale). He hasn't won with a male runner at less than 1m2f since Jeremy took the 7f Jersey Stakes in 2006.

Stoute's haul of ten winners in the Hardwicke is the biggest number for any trainer in the modern era in a Group race at this meeting. He has also won the Duke of Edinburgh six times from 18 runners since 1998. Banking in either of those two events for that record-breaking winner would be sound policy.

LOOK TO
STOUTE'S OLDER
HORSES OVER 1M4F

TOP TIPS

TAKE NOTE OF HIS
FILLIES BELOW
GROUP 1 LEVEL

10	**75**	**6**	**8**
WINS IN THE HARDWICKE – HIS MOST SUCCESSFUL RACE	ROYAL ASCOT WINNERS	WINNERS PRICED BIGGER THAN 12-1	SUCCESSFUL FAVOURITES AMONG LAST 13 WINNERS

Power and the glory

Royal Ascot is one of the key race meetings for Godolphin, rivalled only by the Dubai World Cup Carnival in terms of importance, and there has been a resurgence for Sheikh Mohammed's massive operation in recent years, as well as a change of tack.

The royal meeting offers Godolphin the opportunity to promote Dubai and future stallion prospects to a worldwide audience. Nearly 100 runners represented Sheikh Mohammed, his family or

his friends at Royal Ascot last year, with Godolphin silks carried for a range of trainers after additional horses were purchased in the run-up to the meeting.

Most of Godolphin's ammunition is supplied by their two private trainers, Saeed Bin Suroor *(below, left)* and Charlie Appleby *(below)*, who were both on the scoresheet at Royal Ascot in 2017, but increasingly other trainers have become involved.

Whereas for many years Bin Suroor flew the flag alone, four trainers had winners for

Godolphin in 2016 and last year that number increased again to five (Richard Fahey, Richard Hannon and Roger Charlton, along with Bin Suroor and Appleby).

Perhaps the 'outside' trainers can be more selective with their runners and it is notable that they supplied 16 contenders last year for three winners, two seconds, a third and two fourths.

Bin Suroor has been leading trainer at Royal Ascot four times and his strength has been older horses, with only three of his 36 winners coming in two-year-old races. Two of those three juvenile wins were in the Chesham Stakes, so note any runners there.

Handicaps have recently become a happy hunting ground for Bin Suroor and Appleby, often at generous odds. Steady Pace (16-1), Rare Rhythm (20-1), First Nation (8-1) and Blair House (16-1) all won or were placed in handicaps for Appleby or Bin Suroor at last year's meeting.

'OUTSIDE' TRAINERS DID WELL LAST YEAR

TOP TIPS

HANDICAPPERS OFTEN SCORE AT GOOD ODDS

The Royal Hunt Cup, King George V Stakes and Duke of Edinburgh Stakes are the three handicaps particularly worth focusing on with the two Godolphin trainers. In the last five years, they have had nine horses win or place in these three races at an average SP of 13.5-1.

Appleby in particular is often strongly represented in the two-year-old races. Last year Sound And Silence led home a 1-2 in the Windsor Castle Stakes, Masar was placed in the Chesham Stakes and Aqabah ran with great credit to be fifth in the Coventry Stakes. That was from just six juvenile runners for Appleby.

Sheikh Mohammed's Godolphin had a one-two in last season's Windsor Castle Stakes with Sound And Silence beating Roussel (above)

Major player

J ohn Gosden has played a winning hand at nearly every Royal Ascot since his first success in 1990, missing out only in 2003, but after many years when the winners came in singles he has become a stronger force in the current decade.

The Newmarket trainer had a personal-best of five winners in 2012 and went close to that with four in 2014, while the last three years (as well as 2011) have brought a pair of winners each time. The eight Royal Ascots since 2010 have produced 19 winners for his Clarehaven stable, taking his overall score to 43 (behind only Sir Michael Stoute and Aidan O'Brien among current trainers).

Given that Gosden has plenty of runners, the key for punters is to find ways of narrowing the focus.

One angle is that his record with fancied runners is pretty good. Since 2010, 11 of his 19 winners have been priced at 6-1 or below, from 31 runners in that category (35%, +13.73pt). Much of

the profit comes from his standout year in 2012, although there has not been a significant loss in any of those years by following his shorter-priced runners.

It is worth noting that all but one of Gosden's other eight winners since 2010 were priced at 8-1 to 12-1 (and all in that price bracket were in the first six in the betting market), emphasising that it is rare for him to win with an outsider.

Gosden is known for his patient handling of horses and it is often a good sign when he has a two-year-old ready for the meeting. He has had just 11 juvenile runners since 2010 but four have won, at 9-4, 7-4, 10-1 and 20-1 (36%, +27pt).

PAY CLOSE ATTENTION TO RUNNERS AT 6-1 OR BELOW

TOP TIPS

LOOK OUT FOR TWO-YEAR-OLDS

Mark Johnston

Marathon man

STRONG ACROSS THE BOARD AT 1M4F-PLUS

TOP TIPS

JOE FANNING IS THE KEY RIDER IN THOSE RACES

Mark Johnston may not save his horses for Royal Ascot – famously his stable's motto is 'always trying' – but over the years he has been highly competitive in this toughest of arenas, with 13 winners at the past ten meetings and just three blank years in that period.

With 41 winners, Johnston is fourth on the list of top current trainers at Royal Ascot with only Sir Michael Stoute, Aidan O'Brien and John Gosden ahead of him.

His first Royal Ascot winner came at the highest level with popular stayer Double Trigger in the 1995 Gold Cup and later that day he added a second when Diaghilef took the King George V Handicap.

Those victories at 2m4f and 1m4f respectively set the mould, as most of Johnston's success at the meeting has come in the longer-distance events. He has added two more wins in the Gold Cup and his score in the King George V now stands at five, alongside multiple victories in the Hardwicke Stakes (four times), Duke of Edinburgh Handicap (three), Queen's Vase (seven), King Edward VII Stakes (three) and Queen Alexandra Stakes (two).

Twenty-eight of his 41 winners have been at 1m4f-plus, including last year's two victories with Permian (King Edward VII, 1m4f) and Oriental Fox (Queen Alexandra, 2m5½f). Those two winners came from nine runners over 1m4f-plus (22%, +9pt).

In the past decade, ten of Johnston's 83 runners at 1m4f have been successful (12%, +2.5pt). What is most notable is that six of those winners were ridden by Joe Fanning from 28 rides (21%, +28.5pt).

Oriental Fox lands last year's Queen Alexandra Stakes for Mark Johnston

ROYAL ASCOT 2017

LONGINES

4:49.

American express

Wesley Ward was a virtual unknown on this side of the Atlantic before he took Royal Ascot by storm in 2009 with lightning-fast two-year-old winners Jealous Again (Queen Mary Stakes) and Strike The Tiger (Windsor Castle).

The American trainer had seven runners that year at his first Royal Ascot and, with Cannonball going close in second in the Golden Jubilee Stakes (now Diamond Jubilee), he announced his arrival in no uncertain fashion.

He has missed only one year since and, although he had to wait until 2013 to strike again, he has continued to leave a significant imprint. His total now stands at nine, a score bettered by only a dozen current British or Irish trainers.

Ward has compiled that enviable record from only 47 runners, with his biggest team numbering ten last year, and those nine winners give him a 19 per cent strike-rate and a level-stake profit of +51pt.

The bulk of his runners and most of his success has been in two-year-old races (6-37, 16%, +20.5pt) but last year he achieved a couple of notable firsts.

The 2016 Queen Mary Stakes winner Lady Aurelia scored a brilliant victory in the King's Stand Stakes, making her the first juvenile winner Ward has brought back for more success, and Con Te Partiro's 20-1 win in the Sandringham was the trainer's first in a handicap.

Con Te Partiro was further evidence that Ward's runners should not be ignored at any price, although his growing reputation has seen most of his more recent winners go off at shorter odds. His six outright favourites have finished 011012 (50%, +5pt) and overall six of his nine winners have been 13-2 or shorter.

Ward has quickly accumulated an enviable record at the meeting

FAST TWO-YEAR-OLDS ARE HIS SPECIALITY

TOP TIPS

WINNERS TEND TO BE WELL BACKED NOWADAYS

Richard Hannon

Wizard with two-year-olds

Richard Hannon got on the Royal Ascot scoreboard at the very first attempt when Toronado took the Queen Anne Stakes, the opening race of the rookie trainer's 2014 debut at the meeting after taking over from his father, Richard snr.

He added another winner that week when Baitha Alga landed the Norfolk Stakes and ended his first season as British champion trainer, succeeding his father as title-holder.

His Royal Ascot score now stands at five after two more winners in 2015 and last year's memorable success with Barney Roy in the St James's Palace Stakes, making it clear that the stable will continue to be a formidable force at the meeting.

It is difficult to gauge a pattern after only four years, but Hannon has followed his father's example of producing early two-year-olds and that is one area worth exploring.

Two of his five Royal Ascot winners have been in that age bracket and both were fancied – Baitha Alga was 8-1 and Illuminate was 4-1 favourite in the 2015 Albany Stakes. The stable

has a lot of two-year-old runners, but the dozen who started under 10-1 have yielded two wins, three seconds and a third (17%, +2pt).

Hannon has had only a handful of favourites at this competitive meeting but the market has proved a good indicator of stable confidence, with his four Group-race favourites producing two wins and a

third. He has had two handicap favourites and one of them, Windshear at 4-1 in the 2014 King George V Handicap, was beaten three-quarters of a length into second by the other joint-favourite in the race.

It is also worth noting that Hannon has yet to win a race beyond a mile at the meeting.

TOP TIP

LOOK OUT FOR FANCIED TWO-YEAR-OLDS AND FAVOURITES IN GENERAL

The world's greatest

The biggest races at the biggest meetings are what make Ryan Moore tick and Royal Ascot is the perfect stage for the man recognised as the greatest jockey in the world.

Titles and records don't interest Moore, who has become the go-to jockey for trainers across the globe in Group 1 races.

The tactically astute Moore's strong suit is that he hardly ever makes a riding error. He is supremely confident in his own ability and the melting pot of a meeting like Royal Ascot seemingly has no effect on his ice-cool demeanour. In a nutshell, he's the complete rider, often paired with the best horse in a race as a consequence.

Unsurprisingly, the best in the business is the best at Royal Ascot and Moore's winning record at the meeting over the past five years towers head and shoulders above his rivals.

He has won on 30 of his 146 rides in that time, with a further 36 finishing second or third. That

MOST SUCCESSFUL RACES

Hardwicke Stakes
■■■■
Ascot Handicap
■■■
Chesham Stakes
■■■
Duke of Edinburgh Handicap
■■■
Queen Alexandra Stakes
■■■
Queen's Vase
■■■

2008
YEAR OF FIRST ROYAL ASCOT WINNER

MOORE'S WINNERS BY TRAINER

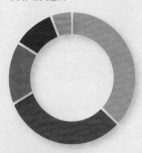

■ Aidan O'Brien **18**
■ Sir Michael Stoute **16**
■ Willie Mullins **5**
■ William Haggas **2**
■ Others **7***

*One each for Clive Brittain, Henry Candy, John Gosden, Mark Johnston, Gary Moore, David Wachman, Wesley Ward

means a whopping 45 per cent of Moore's rides at Royal Ascot since 2013 have finished in the top three and 21 per cent were winners.

He set a new post-war record of nine winners for a single Royal Ascot meeting in 2015 and has been crowned leading rider seven times in all, including in each of the last four years.

Of the riders at this year's meeting, only Frankie Dettori, with vastly more experience, has partnered more winners at Royal Ascot, although the gap between the pair is only eight (56-48).

Seventeen of Moore's 30 winners in the last five years have been favourites, with only three returned at double-figure odds. His biggest-priced winner at Royal Ascot came in last year's Norfolk Stakes aboard 14-1 shot Sioux Nation.

Moore has landed eight of the 36 Group 1 races he has contested at the royal meeting since 2013,

although a level-stakes loss of -10.54pt means backing him blind at the top level would have left you out of pocket.

A better tactic would have been to support him in races below Group level, where his 59 rides returned a level-stake profit of +10.11pt.

Another angle to profit from Moore's expertise is when he teams up with top jumps trainer Willie Mullins at the meeting. They have combined eight times since 2012 for five victories, returning a level-stake profit of +19.5pt.

48 ROYAL ASCOT WINNERS

26 DIFFERENT RACES WON

9 WINNERS IN 2015, A POST-WAR RECORD

TOP TIP
WATCH OUT FOR HIS RIDES IN LISTED RACES AND HANDICAPS

Crowd-pleaser extraordinaire

Frankie Dettori's name has been inextricably linked with Ascot ever since the 'Magnificent Seven' of 1996 and his impressive record at the royal meeting has made his crowd-pleasing flying dismount a regular sight.

He rode his first Royal Ascot winner in 1990 at the age of 19 and his score now stands at 56 wins, with only six blank years in the near three decades since then. While he will almost certainly be overtaken one day by Ryan Moore and has not won the meeting's top jockey award since 2004, he is still by some way the meeting's most successful current rider.

Dettori had one of his blank years in 2017 but only because he missed Royal Ascot with an arm injury. Among the rides he missed were Lady Aurelia in the King's Stand Stakes and Big Orange in the Gold Cup – two of the most memorable winners of the meeting.

He has Al Shaqab to thank for four of his nine Royal Ascot winners since the end of his association with Godolphin, but the owner's diminished British presence in 2018 means

MOST SUCCESSFUL RACES

Queen Anne Stakes
■■■■■
Ribblesdale Stakes
■■■■■
Gold Cup
■■■■■
Chesham Stakes
■■■■
King Edward VII Stakes
■■■■
Prince of Wales's Stakes
■■■
Sandringham Handicap
■■■

that connection is unlikely to be so fruitful now.

However, he is likely to remain first choice when available for Wesley Ward, for whom he has won the Diamond Jubilee on Undrafted and the Queen Mary on the brilliant Lady Aurelia, and the connection with John Gosden, with whom he first combined successfully in 1997, is stronger than ever. At Dettori's last three

1990
YEAR OF FIRST ROYAL ASCOT WINNER

meetings, he has had eight rides at 6-1 or lower for Ward and Gosden and they have included two winners and a second.

Dettori is bound to be in demand when not riding for Al Shaqab, Ward or Gosden. With the possible exception of Moore, there is no rider that most owners and trainers would sooner have on their side on the big stage than Dettori, who remains a consummate judge of pace and as tactically aware as any.

Dettori's 29 wins up the straight compared to 27 on the round course suggests he rides them equally well. Similarly, while there has been plenty of success in sprints, Dettori's five Gold Cups confirm he is just as good over extreme distances.

Only ten wins have been in handicaps, but that's not a bad strike-rate considering they are invariably much more open than Group races.

TOP TIP

KEEP AN
EYE ON FANCIED
RUNNERS FOR
JOHN GOSDEN AND
WESLEY WARD

22
ASCOTS
AT WHICH
DETTORI HAS
BEEN ON THE
SCOREBOARD

7
WINNERS IN
1998 – HIS
BEST YEAR

1
DUAL WINNER
(DRUM TAPS,
GOLD CUP
1992-93)

25
DIFFERENT
RACES
WON

56
ROYAL ASCOT
WINNERS

Reliable and profitable

William Buick has been on the scoreboard at Royal Ascot in every year since 2011 and his record at the past five meetings (12 wins from 120 rides) is bettered only by Ryan Moore.

Last year Godolphin's retained jockey had four winners from 24 rides – a 17 per cent strike-rate – and for backers that yielded a 23.1pt level-stake profit on all his rides. Apart from Ribchester, who was 11-10 favourite for the Queen Anne Stakes, his other three winners in 2017 scored at prices of 6-1, 16-1 and 20-1.

Most of Buick's early success came from his fruitful partnership with John Gosden (11 winners in four years from 2011) but that has dried up since Buick donned Godolphin blue and Frankie Dettori became Gosden's main jockey, and now Charlie Appleby is the most likely source of winners.

At the past three meetings Buick is 4-36 (11%, +18.5pt) for Appleby, although the profit figure stems mainly from last year's winners at 16-1 and 20-1.

With Appleby's yard in such good form this year, Buick is a lively outside

chance for the leading jockey award.

It is worth noting any call-ups by Mark Johnston, who has provided two winners from eight rides at the past three meetings (25%, +6pt). Those winners were two of the only three Johnston rides priced at under 10-1, so the market is a good guide with this link-up.

The Group 1 races are one area where Buick has yet to make a consistent mark, with just three winners at that level, and Ribchester is his only Group 1 scorer in 15 rides since the partnership with Gosden ended.

Buick arrives in the winner's enclosure last year with Ribchester

TOP TIP

CHECK OUT HIS RIDES FOR CHARLIE APPLEBY AND MARK JOHNSTON

James Doyle

Man for the big occasion

I n 2013 James Doyle enjoyed a breakthrough treble at Royal Ascot, headed by Al Kazeem's victory in the Prince of Wales's Stakes, and has continued to impress on the big occasion. At the five meetings since 2013, he is fourth on the jockeys' list with eight winners (behind only Ryan Moore, William Buick and Frankie Dettori).

Last year the Godolphin jockey proved his worth at the top level again with Group 1 wins on Barney Roy (5-2) and Big Orange (5-1) – as a late replacement for Dettori – from seven rides in that category.

Like many up-and-coming riders, Doyle's early chances in the big races were mainly on second-strings and outsiders but the quality of his rides is improving fast and his record on Group 1 mounts at Royal Ascot priced at under 10-1 now stands at 115220110 (44%, +5.98pt).

In fact, he is generally reliable on any fancied horse. Since 2013 he has had 30 rides under 10-1 and five have won, with a further 13 in second or third. That's a 17 per cent winning strike-rate, and a

60 per cent strike-rate in the first three.

Another mark of his growing reputation is that his eight Royal Ascot winners have come for eight different trainers, although two of the last three have come in Godolphin colours and that link clearly provides his best opportunities.

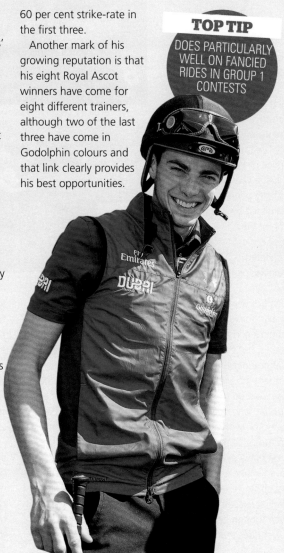

TOP TIP

DOES PARTICULARLY WELL ON FANCIED RIDES IN GROUP 1 CONTESTS

A force at every level

Adam Kirby will never forget Royal Ascot 2016, when he won the King's Stand Stakes on Profitable just hours after his partner Megan had given birth to a son and then 24 hours later he gained a second Group 1 of the week with the unexpected success of My Dream Boat in the Prince of Wales's Stakes.

Kirby scores on My Dream Boat (above, 2) and Profitable (left) in 2016

Just a year earlier he had unfairly been dismissed by one of the sport's most respected trainers for the "all-weather winter tactics" he had employed in the Hardwicke Stakes, but that is now all water under the bridge for a rider who prefers to let his riding do the talking but has long been a force to reckon with at any level on turf.

He has proved that with seven winners across the last six Royal Ascots since his first success in 2012, even though he has had fewer rides than most of the jockeys near the top of the list. His strike-rate is ten per cent and remarkably he shows a +12pt profit on all mounts in that period.

TOP TIP

BEAR HIM IN MIND WHEN HE'S RIDING IN RACES ON ASCOT'S STRAIGHT COURSE

While it is true that Kirby steals plenty of races every winter through his sharp tactical awareness on the turning all-weather tracks, his Royal Ascot record suggests he is particularly effective on the straight course, where he combines good judgement of pace with great strength in the saddle.

His first four Royal Ascot winners, including a Norfolk Stakes on Reckless Abandon and a Diamond Jubilee on Lethal Force, were all in races run on the straight course, and last year he added another sprint on Heartache in the Queen Mary.

Clive Cox remains Kirby's main supporter – the pair will be hoping for another major sprint success with Harry Angel – but Kirby rides for a wide range of trainers, albeit only at 9st and above.

Jamie Spencer

Master of the late charge

Whether you love his style of riding or hate it, there is no denying Jamie Spencer is a jockey who has mastered the art of winning at Royal Ascot.

Day in, day out, Spencer is renowned for his play-it-late style. Sometimes it pays off, other times it ends in disaster, but on Ascot's uphill straight course he seems to have worked out exactly when to make up ground from the rear to give his partner the optimum chance of success.

He was the meeting's top jockey in 2006 with four winners and only Frankie Dettori and Ryan Moore among the current crop of riders have partnered more Royal Ascot winners than Spencer, who has 24 in total.

It is over Ascot's straight mile, especially in the week's handicaps, where Spencer really shines and anyone backing his mounts blind in those races at last year's meeting

There's no better rider over Ascot's straight mile than Spencer – as he showed last year when scoring on Con Te Partiro (below right)

would have been quids in as he delivered a 20-1 success on Con Te Partiro in the Sandringham Handicap and followed up with 25-1 shot Bless Him in the Britannia Handicap.

It may on the face of it seem counterintuitive to suggest Spencer's rides on the straight course should be of greater interest to punters in races with huge fields given the extra competition, but his stats suggest this is the case.

Since 2006, in mile or shorter races at all of Ascot's fixtures, his rides in fields of 16-plus runners have shown a huge profit of +108pt (20 wins from 146 rides, 14%).

TOP TIP

TAKE NOTE WHEN HE RIDES IN FIELDS WITH 16 OR MORE RUNNERS ON THE STRAIGHT COURSE

Trainers and jockeys looking for a Royal Ascot breakthrough

ARCHIE WATSON

The Lambourn trainer, 29, started with one horse in August 2016 but enjoyed a fabulous first full season with 56 winners. The momentum has continued this term and his Royal Ascot team is set to include smart juveniles Shumookhi and Rockin Roy and stable top-rated Corinthia Knight.

JAMES TATE

Tom Tate trained a Royal Ascot winner in 2012 Royal Hunt Cup scorer Prince Of Johanne and his 37-year-old son is aiming even higher with Invincible Army, a leading contender for the Group 1 Commonwealth Cup. Now in his seventh season, the Newmarket trainer also has French 2,000 Guineas runner-up Hey Gaman in his string.

DONNACHA O'BRIEN

The youngest son of Ballydoyle trainer Aidan O'Brien landed a first Classic at the age of 19 in May when Saxon Warrior powered to victory in the 2,000 Guineas. He is bound to have more top rides for his father, who will have multiple representation in several Royal Ascot races,

and may also pick up some choice mounts for eldest brother Joseph, now training after his own top-level riding career.

SEAN LEVEY

The 30-year-old is a bit late to be an overnight sensation but he had a career-best season in 2017 and his profile jumped overnight with his 66-1 1,000 Guineas win in May on Billesdon Brook. She is now in line for a crack at the Coronation Stakes and Levey can expect other good rides from the Richard Hannon stable.

CHARLIE BISHOP

The 24-year-old has enjoyed a great run with Mick Channon's two-year-olds in flying form and, having had a career-best 44 winners in 2017, he should be past that mark before Royal Ascot. Barbill and Kinks are among his juvenile winners for Channon and his strong link with the Eve Johnson Houghton yard puts him in line for handicap rides on Ice Age (Wokingham) and Count Calabash (Duke of Edinburgh).

From top: Archie Watson, James Tate, Donnacha O'Brien, Sean Levey and Charlie Bishop